AN OFFICER AND A TIGER

AN OFFICER AND A TIGER

Trails of Jim Corbett and Other Tales

Yogesh Chandra

RUPA

Published by
Rupa Publications India Pvt. Ltd 2026
161-B/4, Gulmohar House,
Yusuf Sarai Community Centre,
New Delhi 110049

Sales centres
Bengaluru Chennai
Hyderabad Kolkata Mumbai

P-ISBN: 978-93-5352-562-0
E-ISBN: 978-93-5352-918-5

First impression 2026

10 9 8 7 6 5 4 3 2 1

Printed in India

To my wife
Vandana Chandra

Contents

Preface

There are few places in the world blessed with the type and abundance of tropical forests like those that we have in India.

Right up to the 1960s, these forests were alive with animals of every variety and number. There were deer of many kinds—chital, chinkara, sambar, barasingha and hog deer. There were wild boar, bear, elephant and rhinoceros. India was also home to the golden jackal, hyena, langur, rhesus monkeys and, of course, the leopard, lion and tiger. The sub-Himalayan belt in North India, known as the terai, commanded the bulk of this treasure, but there were large tracts of forests all over the country, particularly Central and South India, where wildlife found its natural habitat.

Only someone who has experienced the deep mystique of the tropical jungle—the shrill warning cry of the chital, the belling of the sambar, the *khor, khor* alarm call of the langur, the loud cat-like *meaorr, meaorr* of the peafowl or the deep roar of a tiger—can describe its irresistible and timeless lure. It was a world set in a magic of its own where nature and the environment blended with the soul of anyone blessed enough to be a recipient of it.

But this haunting utopia was to gradually end shortly after Independence when the pressing need for economic growth necessitated increased agricultural operations and the construction of a modern infrastructure. Large swathes of natural forest were cut down, new road and railway lines were laid through them, and rivers were dammed for irrigation, with reservoirs drowning woodlands.

Above all, human habitation began to encroach into the domain of those living in the wild. Fields rich with agrarian produce like wheat, maize, mustard and gram grew right up to the edge of the forests and drew wildlife in hordes to feed on them. There was a terrible toll on their numbers as they were mercilessly butchered, not only to protect the produce, but also to provide meat to the hungry settlers.

There is always a precarious balance between nature and development. As the latter advances—as it must—nature and all that constitutes the natural environment has to make way for the relentless demands of progress. In India, unfortunately, this has resulted in the loss of some of its finest forest cover along with the game and birdlife that abounded in it.

This author was witness to both scenarios. As a young officer in Uttar Pradesh, I was fortunate enough to see the jungles as they were; I was also part of an administration whose priority was development at all cost. If, therefore, there was conflict between man and animal, as there was bound to be, my duty was clear: it was always man that came out on top. That this was to have terrible consequences for the wildlife in the forests was not at all clear at that time. The conflict between man and the denizens of the forest continued for decades and, in a way, continues right to this day.

The Lore of the Jungle

I first experienced the lore of the jungle when, in mid-1962, I was posted as a probationary officer of the Indian Administrative Service on civil defence training in Bahraich district of Uttar Pradesh. Sent on training with me had been K.S. Narayanan, an officer of the Kerala cadre. The Collector of Bahraich, N.S. Mathur, put us up in a nice inspection bungalow for a week while we were instructed on what was expected of us during our attachment to the border district. We were then sent to Kakraha, situated sixty-two kilometres from Bahraich. Kakraha, where we stayed in a forest rest house, was near the Nepal border, and we were sent there to strengthen the civil defence network in the villages of that area.

Going north from the Sub-divisional Headquarters at Nanpara, we came to Mihinpurwa, a quaint mofussil township that was to serve as the command centre for our training and where the Block Development Office was also located. From here we entered the rich terai forests which the sub-Himalayan region is famous for. Kakraha, where we were to stay for the duration of our training, was ten kilometres further.

Having lived most of our lives in urban sprawls, Kakraha was like a dream to us—a picturesque island embedded in a sea of green, a tiny dainty doll's house, just two bedrooms and a dining/leisure room, set right in the middle of the jungle, with no discernible human habitation around. In those days the road in front of the rest house that led to Katarnian Ghat had little traffic on it, so we very much had the scenic retreat all to ourselves. We had a guard, a chowkidar and a cook to minister to our needs and a jeep came every other morning from the Development Office to bring us fresh provisions and to take us around the villages.

The Forest rest house was also surrounded, as we were soon to discover, with large herds of deer—chital or spotted deer, kakkar or barking deer, and sambar. During the day they rested in the shade of the trees that bordered the area, but in the evening, they would emerge and come to the water-well adjoining the rest house, which served as the water source for the building and its surrounding lawn. The chowkidar would fill the cement drain, which circled the garden, with water and we had a grandstand view of the deer that came to drink from it. They had never been harmed by anyone in the rest house and were thus reasonably unafraid.

But as the night advanced, it became a different story. Throughout the night we heard their sharp cries of alarm, *pukh, pukh*, as they saw or heard some predator or the other. The chowkidar told us that the rest house was often visited by leopards or, occasionally, by a tiger, and that the deer were fair game for both! Therefore, after the evening meal, we were also bolted into our rooms.

There was no electricity in those days and we had to make do with kerosene lamps for light. That was the first time I experienced the serene allure of the silence of the jungle, enriched only by the calls of its various denizens. It was a stillness beyond description. It left an impact that I would treasure for the rest of my life.

Life in Kakraha was quite sedentary and we spent our time reading the required law subjects, writing notes on our visits to the villages, but mostly in soaking up the calm atmosphere of our environment. Our work on civil defence was fairly instructive and we met many people in the rural setting who left an indelible impression on us.

Early in our stay, we met the Sub-divisional head of Civil Defence in the district—a robust Anglo-Indian lady, Mrs Jones—who was the Pradhan of Kakraha village and lived on a farm at the edge of the jungle, a few kilometres from the rest house. Her husband was a driver of an express train in the Indian Railways and Mrs Jones was extremely proud of his achievement. She was even more proud of her daughter who was a champion jockey in the race turf in Bangalore, and we were shown the many trophies she had won.

Unfortunately, her efforts to teach us self-defence were not as successful. She used to conduct target shooting classes for the villagers and when, for the first time, she handed a gun to Narayanan, it was only to find him knocked backwards from the recoil! I did not do any better and nursed a painful shoulder for quite a few days. After that she confined our training to map reading and the like, and to doing physical training with the local boys.

On alternative days, we went to the Block Office to

study community development. This was more to our liking and we learnt all about the kharif and rabi crops, the different varieties of fertilizers, pesticides and sowing techniques and how to handle the new machines called tractors and its implements. We were taken to what were called demonstration farms and learnt how farmers could practise double cropping and improve seed production. All this came to serve us well when we became Collectors some years later.

One day when returning to the rest house in the jeep, we had a puncture in one of the tyres. Unfortunately, the stepney also turned out to be punctured. For a long time we sat hungry and thirsty by the side of the road and were just contemplating a long and tiring walk back through the forest when we saw a vehicle approaching from a long way away. It turned out to be one of those modern four-wheelers you read about in magazines and belonged to a party from Kanpur who were camping at Katarnian Ghat, living in a forest resort on the Girwa River, which separates India from Nepal.

A pleasant young man greeted us and when the Block Officer told him who we were, he was most solicitous and insisted we go with him to their camp almost forty kilometres away. He saw we were hungry and tired, and so, brushing aside our weak protestations—and promising to send a mechanic back to take care of the jeep—he whisked us away to Katarnian Ghat.

We met the rest of his family there and found that our hosts were from the family of Bashir Sahib, one of the senior persons serving the J.K. Organization—a leading industrial house in India at that time. We were warmly received and learnt that the family came to Katarnian Ghat every once in a while and camped there for a few days. I did not know it at the time, but a lifelong friendship was forged on that visit.

Over tea and snacks, we learnt of the family's deep attachment to the game of cricket—so much so that they were the ones to organize the country's Test matches played at the Green Park in Kanpur. Narayanan was an avid cricketer and had captained his school and college teams; he would later also captain the IAS cricket team in the Academy. The pleasant young man who had invited us to the camp was Masood Halim, who played cricket for the state and would come to be the Ranji Trophy captain a few years later. Conversation was, therefore, quite smooth and it was fairly late when we were finally dropped off at our jungle home. But this was not before we were treated to a superb dinner, certainly the best we had partaken of since coming to Bahraich.

There were days at Kakraha when, for some reason or the other, our normal mode of transport, the jeep, would not be able to come to ferry us to our destinations and we had to trudge through short cuts in the jungle to get to the village communities. On such occasions, both the guard and the chowkidar would accompany us, one carrying an axe and the other a spear. These they used to bang on the trees as we progressed through the thick woods.

'Sahib,' they explained, 'this is to frighten away the wild animals that otherwise would block our path.'

Sure enough, one day we came across a herd of fifty or so wild boars, of which at least fifteen had tusks long enough to rip a man apart. We had to silently wait and watch as they noisily snuffled around and dug for roots and tasty morsels and then, at a signal from their leader, disappeared into the forest.

Another time, rather late in the evening, as we were nearing the rest house, we were fortunate to spot a leopard walking serenely on the road ahead, seemingly unconcerned by our presence. I had, of course, heard of the animal's feline grace, but seeing it in real life was something else. Its entire body seemed to ripple smoothly as it walked, a quiet intensity in each step. Then, pausing momentarily and giving us a backward glance, it disappeared into the bush. That night the chital kept calling frantically and we surmised that the leopard was still around.

Our last evening in Kakraha was made memorable when men, women and children from the Tharu community, who lived in the neighbouring village, came and performed their traditional dances for us at the bungalow. They brought their own food and locally brewed liquor that we consumed in huge quantities! The Tharu women, who could drink liquor as fast as the men, caught hold of Narayanan and made him dance with them. Unused to these customs, poor Nari could only look pleadingly towards me for help. But, by then, I had also downed a glass or two of their potent liquor and could do little to come to his aid. The celebrations went on till late into the night and then they all curled up on the verandah of the rest house and went to sleep!

The next morning, they were all gone. Narayanan and I left some money for them with the chowkidar. Later, after we'd gone back to Bahraich, we received a thank-you postcard from the Headman of the Tharus.

After the beauty of Kakraha, our last few days in Bahraich were a bit of a letdown, made exciting only by the fact of one of our batchmates from the Madhya Pradesh cadre, and a colleague of mine from college, getting engaged to a girl from the family of leading lawyers in the town. But that is another story…!

Sunset over the Chambal

Although this is not strictly a jungle story (or is it?), it still bears the flavour of early 1960s rural Uttar Pradesh, which were exciting times in the region.

In mid-1963, as a Joint Magistrate posted in Agra district, I was given charge of the Bah-Fatehabad sub-division, situated to the west of the district along the Chambal River. It was the most backward area of the district, largely comprising the deadly gullies and ravines of the Chambal and known for the fearsome dacoits who lived there. The ravines were so deep and numerous that a whole army could hide in one without anyone in the next ravine being aware of it. This was the reason that it was a favourite hideout of the dacoit gangs, who would elude the police forces hunting them for years on end.

> The difficulties of the police were aggravated by the nature of the country in which the gang operated. This comprised about 5000 square miles of ravines land lying [sic] in UP, Madhya Bharat, Vindhya Pradesh and Rajasthan and watered by the Jamuna, Chambal and

Kuari rivers and their tributaries, Agra, Mainpuri and Etawah being the districts of UP involved. Merciless erosion extending over centuries has cut up the area into deep ravines, these ravines following rough and tortuous courses towards the rivers where they discharge their rain water.

Various branches stem from each ravine, making the entire locality a veritable maze. Except for thorny bushes and grass no vegetation grows in the area, which in consequence is populated extremely sparsely. Thus, the area known in local parlance as 'Behar' affords a natural hide-out for bandits and other criminals, who owing to the peculiar topography of the place can remain in hiding for long periods or move about without fear of detection. Indeed, it is perfectly feasible for a person to remain in one ravine without another person in the adjoining ravine being aware of it. As is obvious, without a guide possessing intimate knowledge of the locality a search for a person or thing in the Behar is not practicable.[1]

When I first visited Bah-Fatehabad, stories about the legendary dacoit, Man Singh, who was universally known in the area as Raja Man Singh, were still very popular. Born in a Rajput family in the village of Khera Rathore, situated on the banks of the river Chambal at the close of the nineteenth century, Man Singh inherited a family dispute over some land, with a Brahmin family headed by Talfi Ram Brahmin who also lived in the same village. Matters came to a head

[1]Judgement of Allahabad High Court in the case of *Tehsildar Singh vs State*, 11 September 1957.

on the occasion of the festival of Holi in 1928. Man Singh's family was in mourning owing to a death in the family. On the day of Holi, his brother Nawab Singh's daughter and some of her friends were returning home after collecting water from the village well when they were accosted by boys belonging to the Brahmin community. Despite their protests, the boys threw Holi colours at them. Angered by this wanton act, Man Singh, his brother Nawab Singh and Man Singh's elder son, Subedar Singh, went to the Brahmin's house and, after heated arguments, shot and killed Talfi Ram Brahmin and two of his sons.

Following these murders, Man Singh, his brother, nephew and eldest son absconded and took to the ravines. But on the pleading of his wife Rukmani Devi, he surrendered before the Sessions Judge, was tried and, along with his brother and son, was sentenced to life imprisonment. Owing to drought and famine conditions in Bah-Fatehabad in 1939, they were released on bail but the ongoing bloody family feud led to the killing of five more members of the rival faction, forcing Man Singh to once again abscond and take refuge in the ravines. From that point on, he led a life of crime.

At the Khera Rathore police station, I was shown Man Singh's criminal record between 1939 and 1955, when he was killed. It showed his involvement in over a thousand dacoities, more than 150 murders—of which thirty-two were of police officers—and numerous kidnappings for ransom. His gang numbered around fifteen and included, besides his brother Nawab Singh and sons, Subedar and Tehsildar Singh, Roop Narain Sharma or Roopa Maharaj, Lokman Dikshit or Luka Maharaj, Lakhan Singh, Madho Singh, Jhanga and a few others.

But, as the Police Inspector told me, 'Sahib, Man Singh was a real hero for the people. At that time of crisis, he used to help those in distress in the whole sub-division and in adjacent areas, distributed money and food, dispensed justice to the vulnerable and respected women above all others. Wherever you go in Agra, Morena or Bhind, you'll hear stories of his generosity to widows, vulnerable women and starving villagers. When young girls were to be married, he used to bear all the expenses of marriage for poor families. People sing paeans to Man Singh for the principles he held dear and never abandoned.'

By the early 1950s, however, police in the three states of Uttar Pradesh, Madhya Pradesh and Rajasthan were hunting for him. A joint rapid action force under Superintendent of Police, Quinn, of the Madhya Pradesh Police was created to constantly pursue the gang and not give them a chance to rest or regroup. A network of informers and spies was established to keep tabs on the movements of the dacoits.

In the spring of 1955, the daughter of Balwant Singh, a cousin of Man Singh's wife, living in Kake ka Purva village in Bhind district, was getting married, and Man Singh, as the elder male relative, was invited to the wedding. The girl's father pleaded with Man Singh to attend saying that it was a matter of prestige for the family. The senior members of the gang were totally opposed to Man Singh's going as the cousin was suspected to be a police informer. But for Man Singh, the family's honour was more important than the police threat, and so it was decided that he and his elder son, Subedar Singh, would attend the ceremony. Before going, however, Nawab Singh and Roopa Maharaj made him promise that he would not eat anything at the marriage venue.

Man Singh took an expensive ornament as a gift for his niece who, in turn, gave him and Subedar some kheer to eat. This was part of the marriage ritual and something which the dacoit leader could hardly refuse. But the kheer was laced with a potent poison and Man Singh had hardly left the house when he was overcome with dizziness and vomiting. Both he and Subedar Singh lay down under a banyan tree but were soon accosted by crack Gurkha troops commanded by Superintendent of Police, Vinod Chand Chaturvedi, who surrounded the area and shot both men dead.

Man Singh's loyal gang, in an effort to recover the bodies, engaged the police in a fierce encounter that continued for hours in the enveloping darkness. However, they were ultimately driven back. So ended the reign of the most famous of the dacoit kings of Chambal. While the law enforcement agencies celebrated, the people of Bah-Fatehabad, and especially the poor, mourned their great loss.

So how do I know all this? Thereby hangs a tale!

One day soon after I had taken charge of Bah-Fatehabad, the Collector of Agra—and my boss—Major M.C. Sharma called me in and informed me that one of my duties as Sub-Divisional Magistrate of the area was to visit the Agra Central Jail every month and report on the security and well-being of the two famous prisoners held there: Tehsildar and Nawab Singh. Both had surrendered after an encounter with the police in 1959, during which Roopa Maharaj was killed, and were facing trial for murder. But the remnants of Man Singh's gang, including Luka, Madho Singh, Jhanga and Lakhan Singh, were very much active and a whole platoon of the Uttar Pradesh Police Armed Constabulary had been stationed around the District Jail to prevent Tehsildar and Nawab Singh from escaping and joining their former comrades.

Tehsildar Singh and Nawab Singh had been housed in separate barracks, but when I first went to visit them, both were brought to Tehsildar's barrack.

Tehsildar Singh was a well-built man. He showed up dressed in a traditional dhoti and angavastra and had a huge tilak on his forehead. He had been spending his time reading from a large copy of the Ramayana, placed on a triangular wooden stand, and rearing two kittens that had somehow made their way into the barrack. Nawab Singh, on the other hand, was visibly old; he had gone blind in one eye, but his voice was as firm as before.

They both greeted me as Junt Sahib, short for Joint Magistrate, and politely answered all my questions about their health and well-being. They asked me whether I had been to their village, Khera Rathore, and Tehsildar requested that if I ever did, I should meet his mother, Rukmani Devi, and enquire about her health, as he had heard that she was not keeping too well. I promised to do so and, after some desultory conversation, took leave of the dreaded duo.

I did go to Khera Rathore on my next visit to Bah and the police escort took me to Man Singh's house. I was quite surprised to see a large and well-maintained courtyard and building, replete with all modern conveniences, and a neat living room with lights and fans. Rukmani Devi was accompanied by her grandson Bharat Singh and was gracious in the extreme. I was offered tea and lassi and some sweets, and invited to come over for a meal the next time I was in the area. I told them of my duties towards meeting Tehsildar and Nawab Singh, and on hearing this,

Rukmani Devi requested if I could take some prasad for them that she had got from their deity's shrine in Bateshwar. I agreed to do so, not realizing the red tape I would have to encounter in the district jail.

When I next went to the jail, I carried the small box containing the prasad and declared it to the guards at the main entrance. The box was taken from me and after a long wait, I was taken to the office of the Superintendent of the Prison. He brusquely enquired where I had got the package from, what it contained and why I had visited Man Singh's house.

I was then a self-assured, hot-headed young officer who thought he knew everything there was to know about the law. I asked the Jailor how he could dare to subject the Sub-Divisional Magistrate to such questioning. Tempers ran high and I demanded to see the jail manual to verify what the rules were in this regard.

Luckily, just then the Inspector General of Prisons was also on a tour of Agra Central Jail and, after hearing both sides, he calmly adjudicated that he would himself carry the prasad and accompany me to Tehsildar's and Nawab Singh's barracks. On the way he gently explained to me that the jail authorities had to be extremely cautious so that no harmful substance such as poison could be passed to the undertrials as they were technically under the protection of the court till their sentences were pronounced. And so it was that the next time I met Tehsildar Singh and his uncle, I was escorted to their barracks by none other than the head of prisons for the entire state!

Tehsildar Singh and Nawab Singh touched the prasad to their foreheads before taking a bite of it, and when

I recounted the brouhaha I had gone through to get it to them, their attitude towards me changed dramatically. Where it had been largely formal before, it became friendly and relaxed now. They were eager to hear of my impressions of Khera Rathore and of my conversation with Rukmani Devi and Bharat Singh. It was obvious that they sorely missed their home and that they could not get enough of it through my eyes and perceptions. They in turn, that day, and on many occasions thereafter, regaled me with many stories of the life and times of Man Singh.

'Sahib, when Daddoo was still in jail, some of these Brahmins—like Khem Singh and Jodha Ram Brahman—who belonged to the family of Talfi Ram, appear to have laid information before the police in regard to the whereabouts of Jaswant Singh, elder son of Man Singh, and Darshan Singh, son of Nawab Singh, both of whom were then absconding. A police inspector, Ramji Lal, laid a trap for the two and in the encounter on 5 December 1937, both Jaswant Singh and Darshan Singh were shot dead.

When Daddoo came out of prison he went after Ramji Lal, the Inspector who had by then been promoted to head of Police Station Pinahat. Every morning, the Inspector used to go down to the Chambal ghati to bathe. Daddoo saw him from across the river and with one rifle shot killed him on the spot. Such was his nishana. Later, Roopa Maharaj accounted for the traitors, Khem Singh and Jodha Ram Brahman.'

It was from them that I later heard the story of the Holi that marked the beginning of Man Singh's career, and of the kheer that ended his life.

'Sahib,' recounted Nawab Singh, 'when the bride herself

offered the kheer, how could Daddoo refuse it, even though Roopa Maharaj and the entire gang had warned him against eating anything there?'

'We tried our best to take away his body,' said Nawab Singh, 'and the encounter lasted many hours. But the Gurkhas were too powerful and we were ultimately driven away. But we came back some days later and killed Balwant Singh, the traitorous cousin, who was the cause of his death.'

'And what about the girl who offered him the kheer?' I asked.

Nawab Singh put both his hands on his ears and took out the tip of his tongue.

'Never sir, never. We were sworn never ever to harm any woman.'

About two and a half months later, I had gone to inspect Police Station Pinahat, and on the way back that evening, I ran into a covey of partridges, which were common in the area. I was driving my open two-seater car and I was accompanied by my official attendant. I had with me a .45 revolver that I had borrowed from the malkhana. Jumping out of the car, I let fly two shots at the birds, but did not manage to kill any. After a cursory search to see if by chance I had hit one, we drove back to Agra.

The next time I went to visit the jail, Tehsildar Singh, after exchanging pleasantries, quietly asked me about my trying to shoot the partridges. Quite taken aback, I asked him how he had come to know of the incident as I didn't think there were any witnesses. Tehsildar gave a wry smile and said,

'Sahib, just as you are concerned about us and come to ask after our welfare, we also keep a khabar, a detail, on you. Do you know that the entire Madho Singh-Jhanga gang, an off-shoot of the Man Singh group, was encamped in the next ravine and, hearing your shots, had come to the top of the hill fully armed, thinking it was the police. Then they saw that it was only the deputy sahib and his chaprasi hunting partridges. They had of course heard of your kind gesture of calling on Rukmani Devi maiya on our behalf, so they did nothing and let you go. Sahib, this is a dangerous area, so please don't do anything like this in the future.'

This was my last meeting with the duo.

Tehsildar Singh was taken away to Naini Central Jail, where he stood trial for murder and other offences. Although he was initially sentenced to death, his punishment was commuted to life imprisonment by the President of India. He was eventually released following the intervention of Vinobha Bhave. Nawab Singh, on the other hand, passed away shortly after due to an illness. Neither of them faced the gallows.

Pilibhit

After doing stints in the districts of Agra, Chitrakoot and Unnao, and a brief posting at the State headquarters, I was at last appointed, in April 1969, Collector and District Magistrate of Pilibhit which, like Bahraich, was one of the terai districts bordering Nepal.

Before leaving for Pilibhit, I was required to call on the then Chief Minister of Uttar Pradesh, Shri Chandra Bhanu Gupta. After making some preliminary enquiries into my past appointments, he proceeded to brief me on my new posting and gave me a very knowledgeable overview of the district and what I could expect there.

Just as I was leaving the room after my conversation with him, he called me back and said, 'Jaane se pehle apne baal katwa lena, before you go, get a haircut.'

Some months later, at the convocation of the Pantnagar University—on whose Board I also served—I met him again and, while passing by me in the ceremonial procession, he leaned forward and said, 'Abhi tak baal achhi tarah nahin katwaye! Why haven't you got a good haircut yet!?!'

My wife and I decided to go to Pilibhit by road, and so, sending our heavy luggage by truck, my wife, my little son, his aayah and I set off in our Volkswagen Beetle to conquer the world. The road to Pilibhit from the state capital, Lucknow, runs due north via Sitapur and Shahjahanpur. The drive up to Shahjahanpur is quite crowded as it falls on the main road to Moradabad and Delhi. But after that, turning north, you encounter the lush-green open countryside and the real rural Uttar Pradesh.

The border of Pilibhit starts at Mighauna and there is a sizable bridge over Raptua River that demarcates the boundary between Pilibhit and Shahjahanpur. As we crossed the bridge, we saw a platoon of policemen, dressed in all their finery and with arms drawn up in the traditional Guard of Honour, standing at the Pilibhit end of the bridge. A huge Inspector of Police, wearing his ceremonial uniform, his Sam Browne belt, and his tasselled topi, waved me to a stop, looked dismissively at my jeans and T-shirt, then at my wife sitting next to me, and then at Vikram and his aayah in the back seat. Giving me a disdainful stare, he asked, 'Barkhurdar, kahan se aa rahe ho? Where are you coming from, son?'

'Lucknow se,' I replied, hoping he would make the connection.

'Tumne koi aur gaadi dekhi raaste mein?' he loudly enquired. 'Did you see any other vehicle on the way?'

'Nahin', I replied. 'Kyun, kya baat hai? Why, what's the matter?'

'Kuchh nahin. Hamare naye Collector Sahib Bahadur

aa rahe hein Lucknow se. Tau tum jaldi se phoot lo.' It's just that our new Collector Sahib Bahadur is coming from Lucknow. So you quickly make yourself scarce.

As my wife suppressed a snicker, I quickly phoot lo-ed from his presence and drove on to Pilibhit.

On reaching there, we asked folk by the roadside for directions to the PWD Inspection House, where we were to stay till my predecessor had vacated the Collector's residence. Perhaps people hadn't seen a Volkswagen Beetle before in the town, but we certainly got strange looks as we wended our way to the official guest house. At the PWD Bungalow, things were again a bit disorganized. Policemen were standing or loitering about; officials were standing here and there on the lawns and some officers were ensconced in chairs on the verandah. I didn't know what they had been expecting—perhaps a siren-blaring, huge official car with a suited-booted, white haired officer in it—but the tiny Beetle with a jean-clad occupant was certainly not what they had had in mind.

A chaprasi wearing the official tahsil dress came up to the car and asked me what I wanted. Having learnt a lesson from before, I got out of the car and, mustering whatever authority I could, introduced myself as the new Collector and informed them that I most probably had a reservation in the place.

The electric effect that this announcement had on the place was not something I had seen anywhere else. The officers lolling on the verandah literally hurled themselves to the pavement, many upsetting the chairs they were sitting on. People ran helter-skelter, shouting, 'Vo agaye hein, they have come.' The policemen fell over each other, righting their uniforms and rifles before standing in the traditional Guard of Honour. A stammering, somewhat rotund officer came and introduced himself as the Additional District Magistrate.

This was my first official introduction to the district!

About a fortnight or so later, and as was the custom at the time, the heads of different police stations came to call on the new District Magistrate. The 'phoot lo' inspector from Mighauna was one of them. Coming into my chamber and smartly saluting, he gave me a long and piercing look.

'Sarkar ko kahin dekha hein,' he stated. 'I have seen your good self somewhere.'

I squirmed in my chair, but then replied in what I hoped was a sufficiently authoritarian voice.

'Nahin, kahin nahi. No, I don't think so.'

What he thought of this exchange I don't know, but when he saw my Beetle parked in the garage, he knew, without a smidgen of doubt, that he had told the new Collector of the district, in no uncertain terms, to buzz off!

The Mala Tiger

The Mala Forest rest house is situated around sixteen kilometres from the Pilibhit Collector and District Magistrate's residence.

The rest house is surrounded by verdant teak forests that extend through the woodlands of Mustafabad and Mahof all the way north to the Sardar Sagar Lake on the bank of the Sharda Canal. To the South and East, the Mala jungles are bordered by rich sugar-cane fields, which grow right up to the forest's edge. The closely packed cane provides cool shelter to all types of game—wild boar, hog deer, nilgai and barking deer. It is also home to predators like tigers and leopards that find in the cane easy prey for killing.

It was a hot day towards the end of June 1969, when a Sardar farmer Zile Singh, cycling home after purchasing cattle feed from Pilibhit, took a shortcut via the road running past Mala. While passing the tall cane fields, he suddenly saw a huge tiger silently disappearing into the cane fields. He quickly peddled home to his jhala and alerted folk in the few neighbouring huts to what he had seen.

It was fortunate that he did so, for the tiger he had chanced upon had been hungry, and that very night, it killed a young buffalo in the village.

Now buffaloes are a precious commodity for the hardworking peasant, and soon a small delegation of the villagers made a report of the kill to the local Tehsildar who duly communicated the same to me.

I had only recently taken charge as Collector and decided to camp at Mala as a way of reassuring the villagers that the administration was sympathetic to their plight. This was my first posting as head of a district, and my first foray into the jungles. Of tigers and the like, I, of course, knew not a thing.

Accompanied by my wife and small kid, we set up camp at Mala. When news of this spread, people from surrounding areas came daily to meet me, giving petitions and seeking redressal of local grievances.

Among the callers was a tall, stately gentleman who was a former zamindar, Kunwar Bharat Singh, who had large landholdings in North Pilibhit. Apart from being a venerated resident of the district, Bharat Singh was a renowned shikari, well-versed in jungle lore and with many kills to his name. Keeping in mind, therefore, the reason I had come to Mala, I requested him to camp with me, to which he readily agreed.

And so began my indoctrination into the laws of the jungle—and, incidentally, also to many of the techniques of local governance.

Being a Collector in those days placed immense power and responsibility on one's shoulders and one had to literally learn on the job. I was fortunate to have a gentlemanly Zamindar teaching me the tricks of the trade: who were the important people in the district and how much one could rely on them; who were the crooks and how to tackle them; which politician had what kind of following and how to get on with them; and when to speak and when not to.

'You have a mandate, Sahib,' he used to often say, 'to distinguish between right and wrong and to dispense justice no matter what the cost.' This was a dictum that would serve me well in life as an administrator.

These priceless gems on the role of the Collector apart, Bharat Singh taught me much about the denizens of the forest and how to deal with them and, above all, how to treat them with care.

I learnt the language of the wild: the *pukh, pukh, pukh* call of the spotted deer or chital when alarmed or in sight of predators; the dog-like cry of barking deer; the *khor, khor* warning of the black-faced langurs; the belling of the sambar; and, of course, the earth-chilling roar of the king of the jungle—the tiger. I learnt to distinguish the trails left by the animals, their hoof or pug marks, how old they were and the directions in which they were going.

None of this was learnt in a day, or even days, but at least I was learning. And this is what distinguishes the experienced from the novice.

I spent many hours roaming the jungle in Bharat Singh's black open-fronted jeep and while my wife and I saw innumerable animals, we were denied a darshan of the tiger himself. After spending a few days in Mala, we took leave of Bharat Singh and returned to headquarters in Pilibhit.

Monsoon was late in arriving and the hot weather lasted well into the middle of July. After a long day in office, I was just about to turn in when a delegation of sardars, not far from Zile Singh's village, came to urgently see me.

'Sahib,' they said to me, 'the tiger has killed a grown buffalo that had wandered off into the jungle. He has eaten a part of it and we have covered the remains. If you come in the morning we will erect a machan from which you will be able to see the tiger.'

They left the location of the kill with my staff and, by mid-morning, my wife and I, accompanied by some tahsil staff, set off for the forest. Bharat Singh was away in his area, so I borrowed a shotgun with ammunition from the police malkhana hoping it would suffice for any protection that we might need.

On reaching the site of the kill, which was not far from the road between Mala and Mahof, we found that the villagers had put up a machan over the dead buffalo which was now beginning to smell. The tiger had consumed the rear portion but there was still enough left to entice him to come again. The machan comprised an inverted charpoi tied by its four legs to the fork of the tree about twenty feet above the ground. Leaves and branches from the tree had been placed below and around the charpoi to camouflage it. On the inverted charpoi, an old mattress had been spread to make our stay comfortable.

The staff had brought two flasks of water, tea and some biscuits, and laden with these, along with the gun and ammunition, a very inexperienced Collector and his wife climbed up the ladder well before sunset to await the coming of the tiger. The villagers and my staff left shortly thereafter and parked themselves on the road, luckily within hailing distance from where we were sitting.

Our first stint on the machan was fairly interesting, to put it mildly. The evening was hot and sultry and my wife kept fanning herself with her chunni. We were soon assaulted by hordes of mosquitoes who seemed to relish tormenting us. Not used to sitting up on machans, we kept fidgeting, trying to find the most comfortable position on the lumpy mattress. Added to this were the annoying blue-bottle flies buzzing around us, attracted by the rapidly decaying buffalo—which was now smelling horribly—lying about fifteen yards from the base of the tree.

Neither my wife nor I was in a position to appreciate the show that was being put on below us by the denizens of the jungle. First a herd of wild boars came snuffling round and seemed fascinated by the dead buffalo. They soon wandered off to be replaced by golden-brown jungle fowl pecking for their evening meal. We witnessed a flock of black-faced langurs foraging among the leaves and, finally, a pair of beautifully coloured pea-fowl came to frolic below. But something frightened them, and they suddenly flew away with their alarm call of *meowr, meowr, meowr.*

Had we only known, this was a sure sign of an approaching predator. But we continued to fidget—until, from a distance, we clearly heard the footsteps of something large trampling the dried teak leaves scattered on the ground.

All of a sudden, the jungle was hushed and except for the sound of plodding feet, nothing else was audible. It was becoming quite dark by now and both my wife and I froze in trepidation. The footfalls were coming from behind us and stopped right at the base of the tree we were perched on.

For a long time nothing happened, and then suddenly we heard sounds of an animal panting loudly for breath. This was happening just below us and the machan now seemed altogether too near to the ground. Yet we could see nothing without leaning over the side which, of course, was out of the question. The dead buffalo lay in front of us, and with bated breath we waited for the tiger—of whose presence we were now quite certain—to go up to it.

Whether by instinct or because it looked up and saw us or heard us, suddenly the tiger gave a loud woof, and we could hear his departing footfalls on the leaves behind us.

We remained frozen for a long time but then I braved the stupor and loudly called out to my staff. They soon arrived with lanterns and lathis and we—a very scared but grateful twosome—descended from the tree still looking furtively around in fear that the tiger could return.

Thus ended my first encounter with the tiger of Mala, as my wife and I, dazed, returned home. And yes, the tiger did return to its prey, and ate the remnants of the carcass—a fact that was duly noted by the villagers when they went to the site the next day.

The rains came late that year in the second week of July. The parched earth hungrily soaked up the water and the farmers busied themselves with tilling their fields and planting the kharif crop, mostly sugarcane, to feed the demand of the two sugar factories in Pilibhit. The forests lost their dull brown colour and the crackling teak leaves on the ground provided mulch to the new green shoots on the trees. Soon, the open jungles too were thick with lush undergrowth that provided cover to the deer and other animals in the field.

As the monsoons continued, it became difficult to travel on the kutcha roads and most forest roads were also closed to prevent damage to them. Normally, therefore, one had to make long detours to travel around the district. But one shortcut remained: it was the forest road connecting Mala to the Sharda Canal and the beautifully situated guest house located at the point where the main canal bifurcated—one branch flowing east towards Kherie and the other branch flowing south towards Hardoi. While touring north Pilibhit, one usually camped at this guest house, which was also commonly referred to as 'Bifurcation'.

Once, when I was returning from a meeting in the tahsil headquarters in Puranpur, I took the slightly slushy forest road to get home. The forests were dark with rain and we could only barely see where we were going. Just when we had decided to halt at Mala until the rain subsided, there was a distinct bump as the car seemed to go over some obstruction. This was followed by a loud roar, and looking back, we saw a big tiger glaring at us through the rain. The light jeep had clearly run over part of it, but luckily for the tiger, and for us, it had not caused any serious injury. After darkly muttering what he thought about careless drivers using forest highways, the tiger slowly turned and walked back into the cover of the trees.

This was my first and rather dramatic sighting of a tiger, and it took me a long time to get over its size and demeanour. What remained with me was its gentlemanly behaviour, for even though we had run it over and must have hurt it somewhat, the tiger did not attack the jeep. Had he chosen to do so, there was little we could have done to protect ourselves as we were without arms or reasonable cover.

But I had, at last, seen the Mala tiger.

My closest encounter with him would take place a few months later.

I was camping at Mala, and after a tiring day of visiting the villages, had just settled down to have a refreshing cup of tea in the verandah. Mala was home to a large variety of birds, and sitting out in the evening was a pleasant experience as one saw and heard flocks of parrots, peafowl, the red jungle fowl, partridge and quail. We had also caught glimpses of the chital that lived, like in Kakraha, right round the rest house, and which came out at night to graze on the spacious lawns. One evening I had seen a sambar in the vicinity and was told by the staff that there were quite a number of them around. It seemed obvious that the deer family treated the rest house and its small human settlement as a sort of sanctuary from the predators that were wary about coming near it.

Not so this evening, as we suddenly heard the loud moaning of a tiger quite nearby, which was echoed by another coming from slightly further away.

The forest staff in the rest house were quick to respond.

'Sahib, it's a tiger and since it is mating season, it is calling to its mate to join him.'

My jeep was parked near the porch. We had already removed its hood and lowered the windshield onto the bonnet to shield ourselves from the dust on the rural roads. Quickly forgetting the tea and refreshments, I jumped into the vehicle along with two forest guards and my personal security officer, armed with a revolver for my protection! With my trusted driver, Chotey Lal, at the wheel, we headed out to where the tiger's call was coming from.

By now he was quite audible and growling more frequently. We would urgently drive on the forest road in the direction of the last call and then switch off the jeep to await the next. In this manner we followed the tiger for some distance until we came to a T-junction. The tiger was approaching the road at an angle to our own position. We stopped at around fifteen yards from the junction and switched off the engine. We waited for a minute or so and there, right in front of us, was a huge tiger the size of a young buffalo.

On seeing us, he crouched down on his belly and let off a deep growl, clearly unhappy at having been disturbed while out on a romantic interlude. In the jeep we had all frozen in silence. This pageant continued for a few minutes. It had now become somewhat dark, so Chotey Lal quietly turned on the vehicle's light, and the beast was instantly revealed to us in its full majesty—his rich golden fur, clear black stripes, two sharp eyes staring at us, and a massive head with ears lying flat against his upper neck. His posture was taut, as if ready to charge. The sudden turning on of the light seemed to annoy him even more. Crouching down even further he opened his great jaws and let out a loud, menacing growl to indicate his displeasure. Just when we thought he would charge forward, he turned away and disappeared into the bushes on the far side of the road. We too waited an instant and then quickly backed away from the site. The tiger was now clearly disturbed and there was no need to push our luck further. So we turned around and came back to the rest house.

The next morning, we drove back to the T-junction to see if we could make out the direction he had taken after his encounter with us. To our great surprise we found that there, superimposed on our jeep's tyre marks on the road, were the pug marks of the tiger. It had followed us quite a way back to the rest house! The tiger was clearly telling us, 'Yes, you can certainly trail me, but so can I. Let's see who outsmarts whom!'

Sometime later when I recounted this incident to Bharat Singh, he was quite appalled.

'Tigers are very dangerous when disturbed during their mating rituals. It is a wonder he did not attack you when you so carelessly followed him. Had he jumped onto the open jeep instead of turning away, there was little that you would have been able to do, service revolver or no service revolver.'

This was advice I would scrupulously follow in the days to come.

This was my last sighting of the beautiful tiger of Mala. Though I kept hearing of its exploits regularly since its territory was not far from where we lived, our paths were not destined to cross again. He did not carry away any more cattle in the area and so was never officially declared a cattle lifter, a fact about which I was sincerely happy.

But villagers like Zile Singh would often drop in to tell me about the animal's latest sighting and no matter the time of day or night—or how busy I was—I would diligently listen to the adventures of my gentleman friend from the jungles of Mala.

He was soon to give us a present we would never forget, which is the subject of my next account.

Raja, Rani and Rati

It was along the same road of Mala, and in circumstances somewhat similar to the running over of the Mala tiger, that I had my most interesting encounter with tigers.

Dr B. Gopala Reddy was at that time the Governor of Uttar Pradesh and in December 1969, he decided to camp for a few days at the scenic canal bungalow of Bifurcation.

It was my responsibility to make all the arrangements for this visit, and required numerous trips to the Guest House to make it ready for the Governor's stay. There is a strict protocol to be followed for a Governor's tour, which includes arranging for proper accommodation for him and his staff, food, security, managing who should have access to him, organizing cultural events, and coordinating visits to places that he wanted to see. All concerned district officers including the Superintendent of Police, District Judge, Civil Surgeon, Executive Engineers of different departments and the District Forest Officer put in their best efforts, and the Governor's tour ended as an unqualified success.

After the Governor's departure, I had stayed behind at Bifurcation to look after outstanding matters and it was late in the evening when I left for home. Accompanying me was my private secretary, Mr Sharma, and orderly, Garib Shah, and driving the Jeep was Chotey Lal. We were going along the Mala Road and being tired after all the hectic activity, I was dozing off on the front seat. I was suddenly awakened when the jeep came to an abrupt halt. Chotey Lal pointed to three pairs of shining eyes on the road that looked like they belonged to three kittens. They remained where they were and refused to move even as the jeep approached.

Suddenly Chotey Lal loudly exclaimed, 'Sarkar, they are not kittens; they are tiger cubs!'

Fearing that the mother could be in the vicinity and could attack, he hastily reversed the jeep about twenty yards and waited. Nothing happened. No tigress appeared. The jungle remained silent except for the purring of the jeep's engine. The cubs cuddled up against each other and remained where they were on the road. Chotey Lal gently moved the jeep forward again and just as hastily reversed once again. Once again—forward, then back. This stalemate continued for almost twenty minutes. All this while we kept our ears peeled for any sound of the tigress and kept looking fearfully back and to the sides, anticipating the tigress' sudden appearance. By now our nerves were taut with apprehension as we could neither go forward nor remain where we were.

Then Chotey Lal did a remarkably brave and, as I later remonstrated with him, foolish thing. He slowly edged the vehicle closer to the cubs, sprang out from his seat, grabbed two of the cubs and returned safely to the jeep! Luckily no tigress suddenly jumped out of the bushes to attack him and we quickly backed away from the scene of abduction.

The third cub, left on the road, slowly walked into the bushes at the side of the road and was lost to sight. We waited to see if he would emerge again, and when he did not, Chotey Lal pulled some bushes onto the road to mark the site and we quickly drove away towards Pilibhit with the two cubs snuggling next to Garib Shah.

While passing the house of Mr Avinash Chandra Gupta, the District Forest Officer, we stopped to tell him of what had transpired, and true to his salt, he immediately left for the site to locate the third cub, which he luckily found by the side of the road.

My very bemused wife got over her initial surprise and found a large clothes basket. This we lined with some warm blankets to convert into a makeshift bed and then placed the cubs inside. Milk powder was mixed with warm water and my son's feeding bottle was used to feed them. They were obviously quite hungry and quickly slurped their first feed, all the while meowing loudly and scratching furiously at the bottle. Satisfied at last, they curled up against each other and went to sleep.

Early next morning, while the feed was being repeated, the District Forest Officer and I called the Director of the Lucknow Zoological Garden to seek his advice on what to do. He said he would come to Pilibhit as soon as possible to collect the cubs but that, pending his arrival, we should be very careful about the feed. The powdered milk would have to be heavily diluted in water and nothing solid was to be given to the three.

That day the DFO had arranged for two elephants from the Department and we thoroughly searched the forest near where the cubs had been found to try and see if we could locate the mother. But even though the entire area was crisscrossed on elephant back and on foot, no signs of the tigress were to be found. In one area of the forest, we came across the embers of a fire and surmised that the mother might have carried the cubs to safety on the road but had herself perished in the flames. Rumours also abounded that she had been the unfortunate target of some poachers but since poaching was not heard of in those days, this theory was also discarded, especially as no evidence for poacher activity was ever found.

It seemed obvious, however, that the cubs were the offspring of the Mala tiger and its mate who we had heard calling from the Mala rest house some months ago, as there were no other male tigers in the area.

Rani and Rati

Mr Gupta had to leave for some urgent work in the forest and so my wife and I were left to look after the three orphans till they could be shifted to the Zoo. This took more than a month and, in the meantime, the Collector's house became a veritable sightseeing place for all the residents of the town who came in hordes to see the three cubs.

Raja chomping on Vikram's foot with Rani behind him and Rati on the floor nibbling Vikram's left hand

It was remarkable how fast the cubs grew and how sharp their claws became! Their sharp meowing soon turned into gentle growls. They willingly ran to my wife when their feed was ready. and of the three, there was one male and two females, and we named them Raja, Rani and Rati. Their favourite perch was among the books on my low shelves. With one swipe of their paws, they would send the books tumbling down and then happily perch on the fallen tomes, as if to absorb the knowledge!

One morning when their feed was announced, only two of the cubs emerged from behind the shelves where they normally used to rest. The male, Raja, was, as always, at the forefront and attacked the milk bottle with gusto, but one of the females was missing. This created a big furore and the whole of the Collector's house was sent into a tizzy. The heavy shelves and the furniture were moved around to find out if she was behind them.

All the other rooms upstairs were also thoroughly searched and even the space beneath the staircase was searched for fear that the cub may have fallen there. Just as we were at our wit's end as to what to do, my wife asked Garib Shah to put back the books that were scattered on the floor and there, below them, was the missing cub, fast asleep. After that, a small wooden enclosure was constructed so the three couldn't go wandering off on their own.

One day I carried Raja down to the lawn below, and placing him at one end, ran to the other side. He came charging at me, bounding on all fours, and then curled himself round my legs giving me nippy bites with his now needle-sharp teeth. Next time round I confined this exercise to a small rubber ball!

All too soon, however, it was time for the three of them to go. The Director of the Zoo came from Lucknow with three big cages and was surprised when my wife offered them the clothes basket that the cubs had got used to.

But they were now in official charge of the cubs and thus the Lucknow Zoo acquired three new inmates.

Unfortunately, Rati died while still quite young but Raja and Rani grew to full maturity. In those early days we used to often go and see them in their new home, and while still young, Raja would come bounding to us when called. Of course, he would be inside the cage and there was no question of being close to him or, God forbid, touching him. But often, instead of just pacing up and down the length of the cage, he would come and sit down at its side and then he and I would have a long talk about what was happening in the outside world and how I was faring in Pilibhit!

Be that as it may, my wife and I would nevertheless get a huge kick out of seeing below their names a sign reading: 'Presented by the Collector and District Magistrate of Pilibhit.'

The Man-Eater of Piparia Kalan

Piparia Kalan was a small hamlet comprising about a dozen jhalas or dwelling units on the edge of the forest, a few miles west of Puranpur, the tahsil headquarters. The residents were Rai Sikhs who had migrated from Punjab to make a living from the fertile land. They had earned a reputation for hard work and sound agrarian knowledge and the areas where they settled soon came to be known as the 'New Punjab'.

The homesteads or jhalas typically comprised a ground floor that housed their cattle and sundry livestock, agricultural implements, livestock feed and other essentials. The families lived on the first floor where the rooms opened on to a terrace where the ladies and children of the house spent most of their time. Each jhala had a courtyard where there was a hand pump for water and a watering trough for the livestock. Each household used to make kandis or cow dung cakes for cooking and these would be spread out to dry in the courtyard.

Most of the farmers cultivated sugarcane as the kharif crop, followed by wheat, mustard and gram sown during the late winter months. Oddly enough, the sugar cane was carried to the mills on carriages drawn by small horses, or tattoos as they were called locally, rather than by bullocks. The farmers told me that this was because the tattoos were far cheaper to buy.

As in most parts of the district, the sugar-cane fields abutted the forest boundary and there were plenty of wild animals that found shelter among the cane. This also resulted in many predators frequenting the cane fields.

On a late afternoon in 1968 when the monsoons had ended, a middle-aged lady was making kandis by mixing chopped wheat stalks with cow dung. Her jhala was near the edge of the forest. She did not even get the chance to let out a squeak as a tiger crawled silently up to her and instantly killed her, dragging her body into the thick bushes adjoining the field. Here it made a meal of her, leaving only some clothes and bones, by which she would be identified later.

When her husband and two sons returned home later in the evening, a search was made of the neighbouring households, thinking she had gone to make some social calls. It was only early next morning that a few splotches of dried blood near the kandis revealed the tragedy of her encounter with the tiger. On the soft, wet mud where she had been working, the pug marks of the animal were clearly visible and the pug marks showed that it was an ageing tigress.

The Rai Sikhs were excellent trackers, and arming themselves with spears and lathis, a small group set out to follow the now fading track. The tigress hadn't gone far into the jungle, eating its grisly meal within sight of the jhalas. The tattered clothes and some bones were brought back by the family for cremation. The villagers ascribed the slaying to a chance encounter between the woman and the tigress and not much was made of the killing.

A fortnight later, however, the tigress made a second kill. This time it was a young Sikh boy who was grazing cattle on the outskirts of a village some twenty miles north of Piparia Kalan. The attack and killing was seen by all his companions who ran to the village to convey the news. Again, a rescue party was organized, and this time, a gentleman with an old breech-loading gun joined the searchers.

Since the tigress had been clutching the boy by the small of the back, a clear blood trail had been left. Going into the shrub jungle, the tigress seemed to have entered a nullah or drain and followed this for about two miles before climbing a small hillock that had a big flat rock. Here it had set down the body and started its meal when it was disturbed by something. This was evident to the trackers when they came upon the rock and found considerable dried blood upon it. Looking up, they saw vultures circling overhead and concluded this was what had disturbed the tigress.

The tigress had then carried its kill deeper into the lantana bushes. At this point tracking became both difficult and dangerous. It was also becoming dark and so it was decided that the pursuit would be called off for the night and resumed the next day.

The following day, however, nothing could be seen of the animal or its kill in the dense bushes, even though some of the best trackers spent the whole day on the field. As nothing came of it, a delegation headed off to the Tahsil headquarters to report the matter and seek help.

Bharat Singh's homestead was nearby, so the Sikhs went

to him and requested assistance. He obliged and went to their villages, where he spent many days and nights without any success. It was from him that I first heard of the man-eater of Piparia Kalan.

Over the next few months, the tigress made quite a nuisance of itself in the area. Two other people were killed while cutting cane. Villagers were forced to organize themselves into tight groups while working the fields and had to have lookouts stationed with weapons to warn of any danger. But even so, at night the tigress began to carry off their livestock causing considerable pecuniary loss. The fear of the tigress succeeded in getting an unofficial curfew imposed in the whole area to the west of Puranpur.

I had planned to camp in this area during my winter partal but was strongly dissuaded from doing so by the venerable Shamsul Hasan Khan, the Nawab of Sherpur, who was later to become the Member of Parliament for Pilibhit. Over a luncheon meeting in his village Sherpur Khurd, he recounted some of the stories he had heard of the tigress and, though he didn't say so very openly, implied that I was too much of a greenhorn to tackle the animal. From his extensive private armoury, however, he presented me with a .12 bore Greener breech-loading gun and urged that I be sufficiently armed while travelling in the tigresses' domain. I insisted on paying for the gun but he would have none of it and it was only after much persuasion that I managed to persuade him to accept a token amount.

Heeding the advice of the Nawab, I camped only within well-secured areas. Early one morning, when I was camped within the precinct of the Balrampur police station on the Puranpur-Powayan road, Bharat Singh arrived with the news that the tigress had killed a horse near Mirpur Ratanpur village, about twenty miles away, and that he was on his way to the site. After much discussion, I persuaded him to let me accompany him. The thana-in-charge strongly protested in the interest of security and relented only when we agreed to let him come along with us.

After a light lunch we drove to the village in two vehicles. Now, twenty miles may seem like a short distance, but there were no roads leading to the place. We had to cut across remote villages and barren fields, some of which were slushy with water, in preparation for the next crop. After enduring a most uncomfortable and bumpy ride, we arrived at the site—comprising a few jhalas—late in the afternoon.

The animal had been killed on the degraded forest land about 500 yards from the nearest jhala and many of the locals had actually witnessed the killing. Whether the tigress was hungry or quite unafraid of the villagers was anybody's guess, but it had dragged the tattoo only a short distance to the edge of the forest before beginning its meal very much in the open.

Inspecting the kill from which the hindquarter had been eaten, it was evident that the tigress had planned to return to it later. Unfortunately, there were no trees in the vicinity where a machan could be tied. Sitting out in the open was out of the question. So the villagers suggested a stratagem that, at the time, appeared quite feasible. A huge cast iron kadhai, about six feet in diameter, and used for boiling cane juice to make gur, was procured and carried to within 500 feet of the dead tattoo. A pit, five feet in diameter, was dug and the kadhai was inverted over it. Earth was patted all over the vessel leaving a gap through which the body of the horse could be seen and through which one person could crawl into the pit. A small bamboo mundha was placed at the bottom of the pit on which a person could be seated.

These arrangements were completed before dusk while Bharat Singh, my staff, the policemen and I had tea and refreshments with the Sikh families. It was assumed that Bharat Singh would sit in the pit for the tigress. However, I was quite determined to get a shot at the animal and was adamant to enter the pit. Bharat Singh and the thana-in-charge were, however, aghast at this suggestion and did all they could to dissuade me, but I was obstinate and, ultimately, seeing my determination, they acquiesced reluctantly.

And so it was that, taking my newly acquired gun and ammunition and a flask of water, I crawled into the makeshift trap, sat on the mundha and awaited the coming of the beast. I stuck the barrel of the gun out through the hole in front of me through which I could clearly see the kill. The pit in which I was sitting was about 200 yards from the nearest jhala, on the terrace of which were sitting the rest of the party and awaiting the coming of the night.

It was the third week of October and the weather was still unusually warm. After only half an hour on my perch, I began to feel the heat—the pit was enclosed on all sides and there was no cross-ventilation. The cast iron kadhai generated its own heat and I was slowly drenched in perspiration, forcing me to take off my shirt. But by now a swarm of mosquitoes had also found their way into the pit and so I was compelled to put my shirt on again. All this created quite a commotion since I had to let go of the gun every time I changed my apparel. All thought of the tigress vanished from my mind and I was wholly absorbed by the desire to somehow get out of that merciless pit and breathe in the open again.

I don't know how long this situation lasted but then, with single-minded resolve, I banged on the kadhai above me with the butt of my gun, clawed furiously at the mud to widen the front opening, and somehow managed to slowly emerge from the hell-hole of the pit. Luckily there was no tigress sitting on top of the kadhai to pounce on me as I came out, and shouting and singing at the top of my voice, slunk forward in the darkness towards the jhala. Bharat Singh and the others had, of course, heard my banging and the noise I was making, and came rushing down with lanterns to escort me up to the terrace where they had been waiting.

While I took huge gulps of the water and tea that was proffered, I tried to salvage some dignity by giving an exaggerated account of my experience in that God-awful pit. I don't know how much of what I said was believed by the assembled crowd, but all seemed to be of the opinion that I had made a providential escape in coming out from under the kadhai.

'Sahib, this tigress is a man-eater and not afraid of anything. Had it been anywhere in the vicinity it would certainly have attacked you.'

And so, a foolhardy act was converted into a brave, if risky, one and I was saved any further ignominy.

Early next morning, the villagers reported that the tigress had indeed come and dragged the tattoo to the very edge of the forest where it had eaten most but not all of it. There were quite a few trees near the kill and plans were made to tie a machan on one of them. However, whilst we were in the middle of our ablutions, news came over the police wireless that I would have to attend a meeting in Lucknow the next day. So I had to rush back to Pilibhit to catch the night train from there. It was Bharat Singh who remained in the village to tackle the man-eater.

When after two days I returned from the State headquarters, I was greeted with the welcome news that Bharat Singh had shot the man-eater. Apparently, the tigress had come to its kill fairly early in the evening on the day I had left, giving Bharat Singh a clear shot.

The State Government presented Bharat Singh with a brand new rifle for the act of saving the villagers from a dreaded scourge and he proudly displayed this trophy to all and sundry. I was to learn later, however, that for a long time, stories about how the Collector crouched under an inverted kadhai and escaped being a victim to the prowling killer of Piparia Kalan was told around the villages of North Puranpur.

The Cattle Lifter of Sidhnagar

April 1970 marked the end of the winter camping partal but began on a tragic note in the house of the Collector, Pilibhit.

It was the beginning of summer and the weather was unusually hot for that time of year. Being near to the forest, one was used to coming across all types of snakes in the extensive and stony compound. If left alone, they would usually do one no harm. On a particularly hot evening, however, a banded Krait, one of the most poisonous varieties of snake found in India, fell from the roof of the servant's quarter on a group of children playing below and bit one of them. I had come out of the house on hearing the commotion, and hearing what had happened, I rushed the kid to the district hospital. But, in spite of the best efforts of the doctors there, the child could not be saved. It was a sad event and cast a pall of gloom over the whole household.

Soon thereafter, we began to hear reports of a tiger causing widespread depredations in some of the colonies of Sampurnanagar, a prestigious relocation project of the State Government in the northern Terai. Under the scheme, landless families from eastern Uttar Pradesh would be settled on the vast tracts of degraded forest land along the Sharda River. These were really poor people and the idea was to give them parcels of land, housing and seed money to enable them to start agricultural operations. The project was named after Shri Sampurnanand, one of the first chief ministers of the state. While quite philanthropic in conception, the execution of it did not take into account the character of the beneficiaries who were not used to the difficult operations involved in converting virgin tracts to productive land. The result was that a large number of the allottees soon sold the land given to them to industrious Sikh families from the Punjab who, by dint of hard labour, converted this area into thriving agrarian nurseries.

The only problem they faced was the threat of wild animals, especially tigers and leopards. Still, as long as they were careful and stayed well away from the animals, nothing serious would happen. But accidents can rarely be foreseen. Early in February, a woman who happened to be cutting cane too close to a tigress guarding her cubs was attacked and killed. But as she was not eaten, and since no further kills took place, the villagers moved on from the event without much ado and no action was deemed necessary.

From early April, however, official reports about a tiger having established itself in the Sidhnagar/Bharatpur area of the colony started arriving. It was regularly killing the cattle of the farmers settled there, and by August, almost nine kills had been recorded. t was feared that the settlers would desert the area in fear of the beast, which was becoming increasingly unafraid of humans.

The month of September saw torrential downpour in the whole of the terai and the river Sharda overflowed its banks inundating all the villages in its floodplain. Most of the colonies in Sampurnanagar were submerged by the flood and it became necessary to rush food supplies and cash grants—called taqavis—to the affected families.

The only means of travelling on the slushy, semi-inundated land was on elephant backs. One day, in pouring rain, the tehsildar Qanungo and I were travelling on elephant back, carrying a large amount of money to distribute to the affected villagers. We were going along the mudbank when the elephant suddenly lost its footing in a gap where the river had eaten into the embankment. We fell off and the swelling torrent started carrying us rapidly downstream. We clung to each other, and to the bag containing the money, while the shouting villagers kept running along the shore trying to rescue us. We were swept almost four kilometres downstream before the elephant regained his foothold. The relieved beneficiaries helped us dismount, having saved us from an imminent watery end!

All I was able to think of at the moment was the headline in the local press: 'Collector and staff disappear with money in swollen river!'

The nearest guest house was in Sampurnanagar, bordering the nearby district of Lakhimpur Kheri, and it was here that I set up camp to provide relief to the farmers. After the day's work got over, I would invariably be surrounded by the Rai Sikhs who related stories of their experiences with the wild animals that were very common in the area. Of special mention was the cattle-killer of Sidhnagar, about whom I heard numerous tales—accounts of close encounters that luckily ended without serious injury or worse.

One story went thus: Dilawar Singh, a tall stately Sikh, was cycling slowly back to his farm, leading his cow that had wandered off into the jungle by a rope. Suddenly a tiger appeared from the bushes and knocked him from his perch on the cycle, delivering a glancing blow to his forehead with its claws. The target of the tiger had obviously been the cow, as it left Dilawar Singh to attack the poor beast. Luckily, though bleeding heavily from the gash on his forehead, the brave Sikh was able to attack the tiger with his cycle and succeeded in chasing it away. While the tiger disappeared into the adjoining cane fields, the intrepid farmer quickly got hold of the cow and, heaving the cycle onto his shoulders, made it back to his colony without further incident.

'Sahib,' he said, as he showed me the nasty wound on his forehead, 'had the tiger not gone after the cow, it would certainly have killed me.'

We were soon joined by Bharat Singh who had come to identify the beneficiaries in that colony. He was limping heavily as he had badly sprained his ankle while working on his farm but had nevertheless come to be of help.

A few days passed in distributing the relief money and planning reconstruction as the flood abated. Luckily, by now the rain had stopped and the farmers were slowly returning to their homes to assess the damage they had incurred.

Just as I was planning to return to headquarters, a group of Sikhs excitedly came to the rest house one morning with news that the tiger had killed a buffalo virtually on the road to Pilibhit, about twenty kilometres from the rest house. By then, my jeep from Pilibhit had reached, and after breakfast, Bharat Singh and I left with the villagers to survey the scene.

The kill was lying by the side of the cane fields and under a sprawling mango tree, just twenty-five feet from the road. The owners were wailing over the huge monetary loss they had suffered and a small crowd had gathered on the road in sympathy. I comforted them as best as I could and persuaded them to leave the place, fearing that the tiger would be disturbed.

'Sahib, shaitan ko mariyega zaroor,' they exhorted while going away. 'Please do kill the devil.'

The next bit will seem very strange to modern readers who are used to campaigns to save the tiger. You must remember that in 1970 Project Tiger had not yet begun, and it was often the duty of a District Magistrate to protect local villagers from man-eaters or cattle lifters. Hence the requests from the villagers had to be taken seriously, and I followed the rules and regulations that were then in place.

The mango tree was bounded by the road on one side and surrounded on all others by tall sugar-cane plants extending as far as the eye could see. I was told that the cane covered an area of five kilometres on each side and it had become the home of the tiger during the flood. It had taken to killing livestock that wandered to the edge of the fields, and unless tackled, would cause serious loss to those who had settled in the area.

Bharat Singh hobbled on one foot as he inspected the site around the kill and quietly gave instructions to tie a machan on the mango tree. A stout charpoi was procured and tied upside down on the branches under which the dead buffalo was lying. Bharat Singh himself supervised the hiding of the machan with mango leaves so that it would not be visible from the ground. He insisted on maintaining total silence near the kill, and as a diversion, even directed two men to climb a tree further down the road, and noisily cut branches and leaves with their axes.

The tehsildar had meanwhile managed to procure a .12 bore gun and a few cartridges from one of the farmers. After an early tea at the rest house, Bharat Singh and I climbed up the bamboo ladder to the machan, telling the staff to wait on the road near where the men were cutting the branches.

It was still quite early in the evening and the sky was aglow with pink and gold colours which the setting sun had diffused through the scattered clouds, reminding one of the heavy rainfall earlier. The cane was alive with the cries of kakkar, black partridge and the occasional pea-fowl, while a dog barked from the village in the distance. The whole atmosphere seemed to exude peace and tranquillity. The only jarring note in this symphony of calm was the dead buffalo lying twenty feet below us and somewhat to the side near the cane.

I had just finished checking to see if the gun had been loaded with a ball cartridge when Bharat Singh quietly nudged me. I looked down and there, sniffing at the kill was a large tiger already come for its meal.

How I then regretted not giving the only weapon we had

to Bharat Singh! I had never fired at any animal before and I was now required to take a shot at a tiger! Still there was nothing to be done, so, gently lowering the gun and aligning the bead just below its left shoulder, I pressed the trigger.

The next fifteen minutes are going to be etched in my mind forever.

The bullet made a loud thump as it clearly hit the tiger. It gave a loud roar as it fell backwards, thrashing and tearing at the cane in a fury. We sat frozen in place, benumbed by shock. For some time, the tiger kept tearing the cane with loud and angry roars and bloodcurdling growls—and then, silence.

A silence so pervasive as to be almost surreal.

Have you ever experienced silence after some ear-shattering noise? Like after a jet engine or rocket takes off.

Believe me, it is nothing in comparison to the angry roaring of a wounded tiger just twenty feet below you in the dark.

For indeed, it had by then become totally dark. Where the late evening had gone, I could not say, but now nothing was visible. Stare as hard as we might, we could not see the cane nor the buffalo or the road. Of the tiger there was not the slightest sign and my voice sounded oddly loud as I enquired of Bharat Singh, 'Do you think it is dead?'

Bharat Singh shrugged his shoulder and said, 'You have certainly hit it hard and it is badly wounded. We will, in all probability, find a dead tiger in the morning.'

The problem now was the staff on the road. Hearing the shot and the cries of the tiger they would, in all probability, come rushing to the machan, and if, as we feared, the animal was only wounded and not quite dead, they would be in mortal danger. Luckily, they had also reached the same conclusion, and had come warily in the jeep with all the lights on. We were able to yell at them to stay away and come again in the morning to bring us down from the machan.

On the machan, we spent the whole night discussing the fate of the tiger. Our conversation was carried on in whispers with one ear peeled for any sound from the cane fields. If the tiger was dead, as we hoped it would be, all would be well. If it was not, and only wounded, then we would have the unenviable task of following the most dangerous wounded animal in the world through thick cane and killing it before it became a man-eater. Once again, I wished fervently that I had handed the weapon over to my companion!

Finally dawn broke over the cane fields and we could at last stretch our limbs. Once again, the jungle birds gave vent to their numerous cries to welcome the new day. The attention of my companion and me, however, was riveted on the spot where the tiger had fallen. By then, I could remember, in my mind's eye, every stalk and leaf of the place. Imagination also started playing tricks on my mind and I began to conjure up wholly unrealistic images of the tiger's leg lying frozen among the cane.

Before long the staff arrived in the jeep, and I gingerly alighted from the machan while Bharat Singh stood guard with the gun pointed at the cane fields. He then descended while I nervously kept the gun pointed in the same direction. Chotey Lal was all for going to the edge of the cane fields with the gun but was dissuaded by my desperate plea for some tea.

We returned to the rest house for refreshments and change before coming quickly back to the machan. To my horror the road was by now full of people from the neighbouring villages wanting to catch a glimpse of a 'dead' tiger. The local police had to be sent for to clear the area, as we warned the villagers that the tiger was only wounded and could still be extremely dangerous.

The height of the cane where the animal had fallen was about twelve or so feet tall. It was also so densely packed as to be virtually impenetrable. An armed Bharat Singh and some Rai Sikhs examined the site and found plenty of blood where the tiger had fallen but no sign of the animal itself.

The Rai Sikhs, who were expert trackers, came to the conclusion that the wounded animal had lain close to where it had fallen and had been there all night, but moved further into the cane in the morning when the staff came to bring us down. It was a frightening thought that as I was descending from the machan the tiger could well have been watching me from close by!

So now we were faced with a big problem: how to follow a wounded tiger through the thick cane fields.

We sat by the side of the road to consider our options. The obvious solution was to bring the elephant and search for the tiger on elephant back. However, this was ruled out when the mahout of the elephant emphatically stated that the animal had never encountered a tiger and could be unmanageable once inside the cane fields. Nor was any available vehicle powerful enough to navigate the dense cane fields.

Finally, three of the Rai Sikhs came up with a solution. Pritam Singh, Piara Singh and Dilawar Singh—whom I have mentioned earlier—announced that they were prepared to enter the cane fields and track the tiger if Bharat Singh or the Sahib came with them with a gun. Bharat Singh was the obvious choice—but he could hardly walk and was in no condition to go into the fields. That left only me, and so, despite loud protestations from all concerned, I decided to undertake the task. My main argument was that as I had wounded the tiger, it was my responsibility to ensure his end. Finally, all was settled, and armed with the loaded gun and accompanied by my faithful security guard Bhagwati and his revolver, I followed the three brave Sikhs into the cane fields.

Had I known the peril of the chase I would not have been so foolhardy as to place myself and my companions in the mortal danger of following a wounded tiger. But I was then more than a little immature and emboldened by the events of the previous day. I was also bolstered by the fearlessness of the Sikhs. So, on I went into that dark cane field, listening to the whispered instructions of Pritam Singh, who was by my side throughout, guarding me with a stout spear, as a perspiring Bhagwati followed along.

Fear adds fantasy to any chase, and making my way through the cane, I kept seeing tigers at every step. It was amazing how the Sikhs leading us proceeded through the cane without making a single sound. My guard and I tried our best to put our feet where the others had tread. It was a slow and agonizing pursuit.

Piara Singh, who was the best at tracking, led the way. He would find a drop of blood or a broken stem or a crushed leaf and unerringly guide us on. He would see signs that others could not and continued to find the way even in the deep darkness. We had now come almost a kilometre into the cane fields and Piara Singh signalled to us to slow down. He sat down and motioned to us to do the same and to remain totally silent. We did so and remained in that position for almost half an hour. Through sign language, Piara Singh informed us that the tiger had sat down ahead and that it was now dangerous to follow it further. So as silently as possible, we turned around and slowly made our way back to the road.

The people assembled there greeted us with great relief. Bharat Singh kept saying that he should have held me back by force instead of letting me go on the trail of the wounded animal.

'Sahib, had something happened to you, I would have been put in jail for endangering the life of the Collector. Ankle or no ankle, I should not have let you go.'

The tehsildar and the rest of the staff acquiesced and scolded the mahout for not allowing us to travel on his animal.

Just then a young Sardar, Nirmal Singh, who lived nearby, offered to take his tractor into the cane field and drive it in circles around the tiger. As the powerful machine was driven into the field, it pressed the cane down, creating a path through the fields. With a few of us seated behind him, Nirmal Singh started driving in a square around the area the tiger was believed to be lying, gradually narrowing the square with every pass. Just as the first pass was coming to an end, Piara Singh got off the tractor, and examining the ground for pug marks, stated that the tiger was still within the square.

The area covered by the tractor's passes was growing smaller and smaller. Every successive round of this manoeuvre was, at this time, becoming increasingly dangerous, as at any moment the tiger could spring onto the tractor, taking Nirmal Singh—along with a few of us—down. I had my gun trained towards the front of the tractor, but we were swaying so much from side to side that I had difficulty in just sitting upright, let alone aiming the gun on anything properly.

Suddenly, with a huge roar, the tiger attacked the front wheel of the tractor and literally tore it to shreds. The tractor tilted dangerously to one side and we clung on to it for dear life. I forgot all about getting a shot at it, barely managing to stop the gun from falling from my grip. Just as we were preparing for the tiger to take a leap at us, it disappeared once more into the cane fields.

By then we had had enough. My brave sardars were at this point quite convinced that the Sahib was not capable of killing the tiger from the tractor, and rather than endangering all their lives, they deemed it better to return to think things over. So, we turned around on the tilting three-wheeled tractor and returned to the road.

Not much was said other than examining the shredded tyre and remarking on the strength of an animal that could, with one swipe, cause such damage. I gave to Nirmal Singh compensation for the destroyed tyre and commended him for his bravery in continuing to sit on the driver's seat, even as a tiger was attacking his vehicle.

It was now getting dark, and so as not to disturb the area any further, we got into the jeep and returned to the rest house. The others followed us on tractors, cycles and on foot.

After a refreshing meal of rice and dal, the discussions went on late into the night. Much of this discussion centred on the behaviour of the tiger. Surely he must have been aware of the tracking party following him, for no matter how much we tried, our trampling through the cane was bound to make some noise. The tiger has an unequalled gift for hearing and it was, therefore, a mystery as to why he did not ambush us. Then again, in the evening he could have mauled or killed some of us on the open tractor on which he had us at his mercy. A tiger is known for its ferocity and a wounded one even more so. So why did we get away without a scratch?

Bharat Singh came nearest to the answer when he suggested that perhaps the animal was badly wounded and not in a fit condition to attack. From Bharat Singh's telling, it appeared that this was something we would do well to keep in mind when we set out to tackle it the next day. To my mortification, it was also unanimously decided that I should not be exposed to any further danger and so have no future role in tracking the tiger.

The next morning, and before any of us could get up from a weary sleep, Piara Singh brought us news that the tiger had left the cane and had limped to a pool of water amidst the narkul growing by the side of the road. The Sikhs had risen at dawn and gone to the site after loading their cycles on a truck belonging to a relative. Their intention was to prevent anyone from disturbing the area. As they passed the fields, however, they had noticed the pug marks of the tiger coming out of the cane fields and going towards the water. Pritam Singh and Dilawar Singh had remained behind on the roof of the truck to keep an eye on any further movement, and Piara Singh was sent to fetch us urgently.

We wasted no time in crowding into the jeep and rushing

to the spot that was about a kilometre further down the road from the machan.

Kewal Singh, the owner of the truck, carried with him a muzzle-loading gun, while Bharat Singh was now armed with a gun that he had procured locally. The three Sikhs remained on the road with the muzzle loader while Bharat Singh and I went up to the roof of the truck. Probably because of the excess water, the land near the narkul had little or stunted cane and was more of an open field. So, after driving further down the road, we took a U-turn into the field that brought us next to the patch of water.

Pritam Singh, Dilawar and Piara Singh had meanwhile collected some stones and climbed up on trees growing by the roadside. On a signal from us, they started shouting at the top of their voices, throwing stones and firing the muzzle loader into the water. The tiger came limping out of the narkul on our side. After that only a single shot was required to down him.

On examining the body, it became clear why the tiger had not attacked us in the cane. The shot from the machan had shattered his front left shoulder and left him severely injured. It was for this stroke of luck, which had caused his own end, that we had escaped his fury.

As I stood near his body, I could not but admire the magnificent beast. I was filled with remorse for having been the cause of death of one of our country's finest animals, whose only fault had been trying to satiate his hunger on the villagers' livestock when other game were not available.

Pritam, Dilawar and Piara Singh became household names in our home and spent many pleasant hours playing with our son in Pilibhit, telling him, over and over again, the story of how the brave tiger of Sidhnagar met his end.

Some months later, when I was in Lucknow, I went on my regular visit to see Raja. I was sitting ten feet away from him behind the steel fencing. He had also sat down and seemed to be listening to my account of the cattle-lifter. When I described my deep sorrow at his death, Raja looked at me and opened his great jaws in a big yawn, clearly telling me, 'Ok, ok, so it happened as it was bound to happen. Don't do it again. Now get on with your life.'

An epilogue to this story, authored by a friend and colleague, started doing the rounds of the Uttar Pradesh Secretariat a few months later. The story went that I, as Collector, was tracking the fierce cattle-lifter with a gun when it suddenly turned around, saw me trailing him—and died laughing!

A Thief at Surai

As one drove along the Sharda Canal from Bifurcation towards the tehsil town of Khatima, you could not but admire the sheer beauty of the experience: with the canal on one side and the salubrious forest on the other. Morning or evening, you would see any number of wild animals and jungle fowl crossing the road to slake their thirst in the water flowing in the canal and you had to drive slowly to avoid colliding with them.

Midway along this road, two kilometres on the left after crossing the canal and entering the forest, one came upon the serenely-located forest rest house of Surai. Around the rest house were a few quarters which housed the Deputy Ranger of Forests and the staff of visiting dignitaries of the forest and revenue departments.

Early in 1971, I was required to settle the claims of villagers against the Irrigation Department for land acquired for the Bharamal feeder canal. Since the irrigation officials had to come from Khatima and from the department's headquarters at Banbassa, I decided to camp at Surai to hear and dispose of the claims.

Surai is located near the Bharamal Baba temple, a shrine dedicated to a saint revered by both Muslims and Hindus. Every year a fair would be held here, and pilgrims from far and near would come to offer prayers. Unfortunately, the shrine was located within a thick sal forest and pilgrims often had to sleep out in the open. There had, therefore, been quite a number of attacks on them by tigers, leopards and bears—wild animals that were quite common in the neighbourhood. Forest officials posted in Surai warned me not to venture out too far into the jungle with my family without adequate escort.

Still, we had to pay a visit to the famous shrine, and one morning, early in our stay, accompanied by armed forest guards and some of my staff, we set off down the narrow forest path that led to the temple. The path wended its way through dense sal trees, and on reaching a branch of the main canal, doubled back in a sharp U-turn to reach the temple.

At the U-turn, where we stopped for some refreshments, the forest officials narrated how, just 200 yards from the site, a group of pilgrims had been attacked earlier that year by two sloth bears. The wounded had had to be rushed to the Khatima hospital where one died and another lost sight in one eye. Naturally this information served to hasten us on our way!

The Bharamal Mahadev temple houses a shiva-linga dedicated to Lord Shiva that was reportedly installed at the time when the Sharda Canal was under construction.

To dig and make way for the canal, quite a few trees had to be felled, and in the process, many human lives were lost to wild animals. The construction staff were told to offer prayers to Shiva Mahadeva for their safety and that is how the temple came into being.

The temple also housed the samadhi of Bharamal Baba and a chaddar was routinely offered to the saint. The act of worship apparently led to the fulfilment of one's desires and that was what drew numerous visitors to the place.

Unfortunately, we had brought nothing and had to be content with offering money to the priest who offered us prasad. Then, lighting his chillum, he told us an unusual story.

Apparently, many years ago, in the 1920s, the infamous dacoit, Sultana Daku, used to roam the area and terrorize the Banias of Khatima. Sultana belonged to the Bhantu clan of Rajputs who claimed descent from Maharana Pratap. His forays covered the whole of Rohilkhand. Once, while passing by the Bharamal shrine, he felt an urge to visit the place and was deeply affected by the temple's aura. He spent a few days at the spot and then would come regularly to pay his obeisance. Soon, the site acquired notoriety as 'Sultana Daku ka adda' and the British police who were chasing him laid a trap for him at the shrine.

'Sahib,' the priest told us, 'for his devotion, the deity protected him. He managed to escape to the adjoining district of Nainital, where the British sent Freddie Young, the fattest police officer in the whole of India, to hunt him down. Young finally caught up with him in the jungles around Haldwani, and in 1924, he was hanged in Haldwani jail, while still in his 20s.'

The priest paused for a while and blew into his chillum to get the embers to glow again.

'Sahib, legend has it that he was reincarnated as a ferocious tiger that still roams the jungles he loved so much and regularly attacks Banias. It is known as the Bharamal tiger and I will offer a few prayers to him in your name for the protection of you and your family.'

At this I smiled and jocularly said,

'Panditji, he must be a very old tiger by now, at least 45 years old. What harm can it possibly do us? But I certainly won't mind seeing him and possibly shaking his hand for fighting the British.'

This was clearly the wrong thing to say, for the priest made a wry face before turning away and busying himself with cleaning his chillum while, on a signal from my wife, we made our preparations to leave.

I received an earful from my wife about my insensitive remarks on a subject that the priest clearly held sacred and it was in a sombre mood that the party returned safely to Surai. I later questioned the Deputy Ranger on the subject and he confirmed the story of Sultana Daku's link with the Bharamal temple. He also confirmed that there was a ferocious tiger by the name of the Bharamal tiger in the range and that it had indeed attacked and killed many pilgrims.

'Sir, under the orders of a predecessor of yours, a police and forest party are regularly posted at the temple during the time of the fair to provide safety to the pilgrims. But the area between Khatima, Neoria Hasanpur and here is fairly large and accidents are bound to happen. So, the tiger has acquired a bad name even though there is no evidence that those who have been attacked were eaten by a tiger. The tiger is not even known to be a man-eater.'

Some months later, when we were in Lucknow, my wife and I paid a visit to my wife's uncle, Mr Rameshwar Sahai, who was then Chief Conservator of Forests in Uttar Pradesh. We mentioned our camp in Surai, and to our great surprise, he asked whether we had run into the Bharamal tiger!

'Yes,' he said, 'it is a dangerous tiger in the area and has killed many people. Once when I was camping in Bifurcation, it attacked and killed an Assistant Conservator of Forests about 100 yards from the Surai rest house. There was a big hue and cry after the incident and a vociferous demand was made that it be declared a man-eater. However, it had never eaten anyone and so the State Government refused. Had I known you were camping at Surai, I would have warned you about him.'

Luckily, neither then nor at any time later did I personally encounter the Bharamal tiger. However, for many years afterwards, I kept reading of the tiger's attacks on pilgrims.

During a meeting of the Commissioner of Rohilkhand in Bareilly in December 1969, the subject of the Bharamal tiger came up for discussion, and again a request was made that the tiger be killed. An official inquiry into its activity was ordered and the Sub-Divisional Magistrate of Khatima was directed to undertake the responsibility. Once again, the fact that the tiger had not actually eaten anyone came to its rescue. And there, as far as I was concerned, the matter rested.

Imagine my astonishment when years later as I was writing this story, I came across a newspaper article, dated 25 December 2018, that I reproduce below:

खटीमा में बाघ ने दो श्रद्धालुओं पर मारा झपट्टा
हिन्दुस्तान टीम, रुद्रपुर
Last updated: Tue, 25 Dec 2018 07:17 PM

Web Title: Tiger attack on devotees going to meet fair at Bharamal Baba Temple [sic], 2 injured

सुरई रेंज स्थित भारामल बाबा मंदिर में लगा मेला देखने बाइक से जा रहे बाइक सवार तीन युवकों पर मंदिर से कुछ ही दूर पहले बाघ ने झपट्टा मार दिया। हमले से तीनों युवक अनियंत्रित होकर गिर गए। बाघ ने पीछे बैठे दो युवकों को पंजा मार लहूलुहान कर दिया। इस बीच मंदिर पर मौजूद लोगों के शोर मचा देने पर बाघ जंगल में भाग गया। घटना के बाद मेले में अफरातफरी मच गई। घायलों को नागरिक अस्पताल लाकर मरहम-पट्टी की गई। जानकारी के मुताबिक पकड़िया निवासी इकबाल के साथ उसके दोस्त साहेब (14) और राजीव नगर निवासी मुकेश (18) मंगलवार को सुरई रेंज के घने जंगल में स्थित भारामल बाबा मंदिर में मेला देखने जा रहे थे। मंदिर से कुछ दूर पहले ही नहर किनारे बाघ ने बाइक पर झपट्टा मार दिया। अचानक हुए हमले से अनियंत्रित होकर तीनों युवक बाइक समेत सड़क पर गिर गए। बाघ ने बाइक के पीछे बैठे साहेब और मुकेश को पंजा मार कर जख्मी कर दिया। इस दौरान मेले में आई भीड़ ने शोर मचाया तो बाघ युवकों को छोड़कर जंगल में भाग गया। बाइक सवार इकबाल घायल साथियों को श्रद्धालुओं की मदद से नागरिक चिकित्सालय ले गया, जहां उनका इलाज किया गया। बाघ के हमले की सूचना पर सुरई रेंज के वन कर्मचारी नागरिक चिकित्सालय पहुंचे। उन्होंने घायलों का हाल जानकर आला अफसरों को सूचना दी।

Rough translation:

Three boys—Iqbal and Sahib of Pakriya village, and Mukesh, resident of Rajiv Nagar—were on Tuesday going on a bike to the Mela at Bharamal Baba Mandir. Just before the Mandir, on the side of the canal, a tiger attacked the bike due to which all three fell on to the road. Sahib and Mukesh, who were seated on the back, were wounded by the tiger with his paw. Just then the crowd at the Mela started shouting, so the tiger left the boys and ran into the jungle. The driver of the bike, Iqbal, with the help of the pilgrims, took his companions to the hospital where they were treated. Hearing of the tiger attack, forest officers from Surai range reached the hospital and after enquiring about the wounded, sent a report of the attack to senior officers.

But back to my story of 1969.

A few days into our stay at Surai, and just as I was about to leave for Khatima, my wife expressed a desire to come with me as she needed some urgent supplies from there. So, she did her shopping while I presided over the compensation hearings. Garib Shah, my long-term chaprasi, who was an excellent cook, bought a whole leg of mutton to cook for us the next day.

Laden with the shopping and tired after the day's outing, we were making our way back along the canal late in the evening. Suddenly we saw a huge sloth bear with its cub going down to the canal for water. We stopped on the side while my son, Vikram, who had seen Bhaloo ke Natchwallah performances in Lucknow kept shouting excitedly, 'Bhaloo, Bhaloo.'

After drinking from the canal, the bears emerged on to the road. The mother raised herself to her full height on her hind legs to assess the situation while the cub clung to her side. Not sensing any danger, the mother came down on all fours and the two ambled off into the forest. We drove silently on our way, the only comment coming from Vikram,

'I wish we could have kept the cub. It looked so sweet and cuddly!'

When we reached Surai, Garib Shah took the leg of the mutton to his quarters to hang in the open in order to keep it fresh, since in those days there were no refrigerators in the rest houses. The staff quarters opened on to a narrow open verandah that had horizontal bars overhead to hold the roof in position. Garib Shah tied the mutton with a stout rope to one of these bars, at a height of about eight feet.

The next morning the mutton was gone, and we awoke to dark mutterings from Garib Shah on the low calibre of the forest staff and their thieving nature. Before matters got out of hand, we gave Garib Shah money to procure another leg from Khatima when he would accompany me there. This he promptly did. That night, he put the mutton in a white jhola and tied the jhola to the horizontal rod, this time at a height of ten feet.

Sure enough, however, next morning the jhola and its prized content was once again gone and Garib Shah was left fuming about what the world was coming to if the thief/thieves wasn't/weren't even sparing the District Magistrate.

More to assuage the feelings of Garib Shah than in hopes of nabbing the culprit, we bought another leg of mutton the next day, and this time, the Deputy Ranger and I decided to sit up and catch the thief in the act.

As before, the mutton was put in a white jhola which was hung eleven feet from the ground. Garib Shah sat awake in his quarter while the forest official and I, armed with a strong torchlight, sat in the verandah of the rest house about fifty yards away.

For about an hour or two after the petromax lamps had been switched off, there was complete silence around us. The sylvan surrounding of the rest house was now suffused by pale moonlight coming from a waxing moon, and the trees and shrubberies were vaguely visible, appearing as sentinels around where we were sitting. Far away, amidst the trees, you could hear the ascending call of the brain-fever bird, the papiha, but other than that, all was quiet.

I was just about to doze off in my comfortable deck chair when the Deputy Ranger gently prodded me fully awake. Suddenly, many chitals could be heard calling their traditional call of danger, *pukh, pukh, pukh,* as they warned of a predator on the prowl. We had got so used to these calls that we had begun to accept them as natural. This time, however, they were accompanied by the dog-like barking of the kakkar, and we knew something was afoot.

Suddenly, from the side of the forest behind the rest house I saw a dark shadow emerge and move determinedly towards the staff quarters. It stopped below the jhola and, with a light leap, pulled it down. While we shone the torchlight on it, Garib Shah emerged from his quarter, shouting 'CHOR, CHOR' at the top of his voice.

The leopard, for so it turned out to be, jumped on to a small neem tree just beyond the perimeter of the quarters, and glared at us. In the light of the torch we could see the jhola firmly held in its mouth. Little realizing the danger, we ran towards the tree, making as much noise as we possibly could.

By now all the quarters were coming to life and the leopard, with singular grace, turned round and, descending from the tree, loped off into the forest with Garib Shah chasing it till he was told sharply to return.

And so, the 'thief' of Surai was at last revealed! Garib Shah found his precious jhola at the edge of the forest the next day, but of course the meat was missing. We decided to treat it as an offering to the place and consoled ourselves with the thought that by giving meat to the leopard, we had prevented it from killing one of the beautiful deer around the rest house.

Navdia Forest Rest House

It was some years after I had left Pilibhit as Collector that I again got hooked on the books written by Jim Corbett describing his thrilling encounters with the tigers of Kumaon and Garhwal. It was not the hunting that attracted me as the extraordinary and detailed description of the places through which Corbett travelled in search of the killers. Pilibhit was close to many of the locations that Corbett mentioned and I yearned to go back to them in a bid to follow the trail of Jim Corbett.

As a family, of course, we had kept our contact with Pilibhit and my wife, and by now two teenaged kids, used to go there every winter. The forest department would kindly reserve the Navdia Forest rest house for us for three-four days. This trip to Pilibhit used to come as a needed elixir away from the pressures of Delhi.

Navdia is surrounded by the most exquisite teak forest right up to its now missing gate and, except for the few forest staff posted there, has no habitation to disturb the serene beauty of the place. There is a sprawling lawn in front of the rest house which comprises three rooms and verandah, and beyond and below the barbed wires in front, is a marshy stream that provides water to the building and is home to much of the wild inhabitants of the locale.

On one of our visits to Navdia early in 1985, the chowkidar told us that a tigress had given birth to two cubs just below the rest house and that the mother and her offspring occasionally came and sat on the verandah of the rest house.

Chotey Lal had by then acquired an old jeep, and thus every evening we drove along the road from the rest house to Jamunia Choraha, about 10 miles, hoping desperately to spot the tigress. We never did. Imagine our surprise when, one day after our drive, we saw the imprint of the tigress's pug marks, along with those of her cub's, overlapping with the tyre marks of the jeep for a long way down the road! The mother and family had come for a stroll on the road after we left the rest house and must have hidden on the side when we returned. Such are the uncertainties and thrills of jungle adventure!

During the lazy winter days, we used to sprawl out on the lawns of the rest house or go for walks on the forest road, always accompanied by trusted forest guards. But now, unlike the old days, the forests had totally changed. Where earlier one had to be alert that one did not run into wild animals, now the woods were empty and bereft of any life. Indeed, now one drove for miles without seeing anything but bare forest. It seemed as if the wild animals had been herded away to some secret place.

One morning during our stay, a small tempo turned up at the rest house. Imagine my great surprise and delight when my old friends Pritam Singh, Piara Singh and Nirmal Singh from the Sidhnagar adventure stepped out of the vehicle.

They had learnt through their intelligence network that we were at Navdia and had come to call on us—laden with wheat, mustard and vegetables to last us for months!

Pritam Singh now sported a distinguished white beard while Piara Singh and Nirmal Singh were well on their way to middle age. They were in turn surprised at how tall Vikram had become from the lad they used to carry around on their shoulders. I was sorry to learn that Dilawar Singh had passed away due to malarial fever and that my trusted companion Bharat Singh was also no more.

Over lunch I asked the sardars why the forests seemed so empty. A shadow passed over Pritam Singh's face as he replied,

'Sahib, the wild animals have all fallen prey to shikar. Many big farms have now come up along the Sharda Nadi and they get visitors throughout the year—rich hunters coming from the Punjab, Delhi and Uttar Pradesh. The sole purpose of their excursion is to procure meat and trophies, and the wildlife has been decimated on this account. Almost any day you can see people going about at night with searchlights, firing at the shining eyes of animals and giving them no chance to escape. Where earlier there were large herds of chital, sambar, nilgai, wild boar and barasingha, now you only see solitary animals. The farms have become hunting grounds and the animals have perished.'

'But what about the police and the forest guards who used to protect them in the past?' I asked.

Pritam Singh gave a mirthless laugh.

'Sahib, they are all in this together. They are either too afraid to say or do anything or they are a party to the sport. Why, the other day there was a huge feast to celebrate the wedding of the local daroga's daughter. It's common knowledge that many animals were slaughtered for the feast. Still, many district officers and politicians attended the function.'

Piara Singh added,

'Earlier, the game was plentiful around the Rai Sikh villages but now some members of even my community are charging money to guide shikaris. They say that tigers and leopards should be protected, but how can you ensure their survival when their natural food is destroyed in this fashion?'

The next day, the District Conservator of Forests came to call on me and I raised this subject with him. He sadly confirmed all that Piari Singh and Pritam Singh had said the previous day and added that there were only a few pockets left in the district where wild animals could still be found, and that too, not even in numbers close to what they had been earlier. He did however add that after the promulgation of the Wild Life (Protection) Act by Parliament in 1972, no hunting was permitted within the reserved forest areas. The problem was in the agricultural areas and farms that bordered the forests and where the wildlife naturally tended to migrate searching for fodder and food. Here, unfortunately, they could not be protected.

'Every farmer is seeking and acquiring firearms, ostensibly for protection, but in reality, for hunting, and there is little we can do to stop this as the argument always is that the farmers are saving their crops.'

However, on an optimistic note, the Conservator added,

'We have submitted a proposal to declare this entire area as the Pilibhit Tiger Reserve, linking it with the Kishenpur and Katarniaghat wildlife sanctuaries to the east and the

Dudhwa National Park to the north-east. Our proposal is supported by a study conducted by the Wildlife Institute of India, which found that the Dudhwa-Pilibhit tiger population has high conservation value since it is the only population to have the ecological and behavioural adaptations of the tiger unique to the Terai region.'

The morning we were leaving Navdia, the forest chowkidar came in through the back door and woke us up, saying,

'Sahib, quickly look out of your front window.'

We did so and saw a sight that has remained imprinted on my mind all these years. There, in one corner of the field, framed by the rising sun, was a magnificent chital stag, with an enormous head of antlers. He was accompanied by a hind and her frisky fawn and was quietly nibbling the grass on the lawn. I ran to the side-room to wake the children, and looking out through our window, we exulted in the sight for a long time. Unfortunately, our cameras had been packed away and a precious photo opportunity was lost.

It was only when the trio was disturbed by the forest guard bringing the morning milk on his cycle that the stag gave a sharp call and all three disappeared beyond the boundary.

It was a memorable farewell sighting, and a reminder of the beauty that the forests of India can offer.

The Lights in the Sharda Gorge

On the way back to Delhi, we stopped in Pilibhit for a day to call on the Raja Sahib of Pilibhit, Shri Radha Raman, who had not been keeping well. We also called on the Collector, and while there, I overheard Chotey Lal telling Vikram about his village in eastern Kumaon, Kot Kindri in Talla Desh, which was accessible via Khatima and Banbassa.

Vikram had read stories of the Chuka and Thak man-eaters by Jim Corbett where these locations, and especially Purnagiri, figure prominently and I could see that he was extremely keen to visit these places. It thus transpired that the rest of the day was spent in planning the trip—the route to be followed, places to stay in, provisions to be carried, etc. I was glad to see the young Collector and his wife enthusiastically joining in the discussions and made it clear that, barring contingencies, they were welcome to also join the trek. Soon after, however, he was transferred to another district and so could not join us.

It was in the beginning of 1986 that we embarked on our journey to eastern Kumaon via Pilibhit. Mr Sharma had made reservations in Banbassa, Baramdeo and Kaladhunga and he came with us as far as Baramdeo, or Boom as it was popularly called. For the rest of the journey, Chotey Lal was going to be accompanying us, along with the porters that we had hired to carry our tents and other provisions.

Baramdeo is a pretty rest house nestled against the hill, on top of which is the holy Purnagiri temple. One path, to the left, went to the temple and a narrower one, on the right, along the Sharda River, led to Kaladhunga and beyond. In front of Baramdeo, the Sharda flowed serenely as it emerged from its gorge. It was along the tapering path through the gorge that our route lay.

The rest house at Baramdeo and a tramway line along the rock cliff of the river had been constructed by a forester, J.V. Collier. He had come to supervise the extraction of a million cubic feet of sal timber which was to be presented by the Nepal Durbar to the British Government as a token of gratitude after the First World War. Kaladhunga rest house had been built as a part of the same project. We saw the place in front of the rest house where the timber had been felled. The tramway line along the gorge had long since been swept away by landslides and floods but its remnants were still visible in Baramdeo.

We spent a few days at Baramdeo checking in our luggage, before taking leave of Mr Sharma who was to join a party of pilgrims going to Purnagiri. He would rejoin us at Banbassa. With Chotey Lal acting as headman to the porters, we also set off on the 14-kilometre trek to Kaladhunga. Kaladhunga, in eastern Kumaon, is not to be confused with Kaladhungi that was the winter home of the Corbett family near Naini Tal.

The first part of this journey was through the gorge

and this part required some steep rock climbing, before opening out into a level but narrow path, with the sheer cliff on one side and the flowing river on the other. Vikram was carrying his book on Jim Corbett and we kept a sharp lookout for the place along the gorge where Corbett had camped at night and seen the lights on the opposite cliff.

Finally, we came to a wide-ish shelf where there was an overhanging rock under which camp could be set up, providing, as it did, shelter from rocks that could fall from above. Across the river from this site was the sheer, perpendicular cliff where the lights had reportedly been seen by Corbett and his men. The final proof was this: Around thirty metres or so further along, the track went on to cross a ravine. There the remains of an iron bridge built by Collier—and mentioned by Corbett in his account—could still be seen.

Our men quickly made us a light dinner of rice and dal and then cooked their meal on driftwood gathered from the river. Since we were all tired from the trek through the gorge, we changed our clothing and prepared to go to sleep. But not before Vikram and I had kept a sharp lookout on the opposite cliff for the lights seen by Corbett.

Unfortunately, we saw nothing. Even though the time of the year—April—was the same, we neither went nor returned through the Sharda Gorge at night, which was when Corbett had noticed the lights.

The explanation for the lights was given to us by the temple priests of Purnagiri who later met us in Kaladhunga. Purnagiri, dedicated to the worship of the Goddess Bhagwati and visited each year by tens of thousands of pilgrims, is accessible by two tracks. These—one from Baramdeo and the other from Kaladhunga—meet on the northern face of the mountain, a short distance below the crest. At the junction of the tracks is situated the less sacred of the two Purnagiri shrines. The more sacred shrine is higher up and to the left. Only those whom the Goddess favours are able to reach the upper shrine; the others have to make their offerings at the lower one.

Near the upper and more sacred shrine is a rocky pinnacle a hundred feet high, the climbing of which is forbidden by the Goddess. Long ago, a sadhu, more ambitious than his comrades, climbed the pinnacle with the object of putting himself on an equal footing with the Goddess. Incensed at this disregard of her orders, the Goddess hurled the sadhu from the pinnacle to the hill on the far side of the river. It is this sadhu who, banished forever from Purnagiri, worships the Goddess two thousand feet above him by lighting lamps to her.

While leaving the gorge, Vikram and I confirmed that the place where Corbett had camped was indeed directly below the pinnacle of the Purnagiri temple. Therefore, to the trusting mind of the faithful, the lights on the opposite cliff could well appear to be the diya offerings of the chastised sadhu to the Mother Goddess.

Kaladhunga

Emerging from the Sharda gorge, one traversed a scenic forest road which, seven kilometres on, led to the Kaladhunga rest house. Completely enclosed by the forest, the three-bedroom bungalow had a wide verandah that opened on to gently sloping grasslands that went down to the Sharda River to the east. Beyond the river is Nepal from where the timber had been extracted by Collier. The picturesque backdrop to the rest house is provided by a heavily-wooded ridge of hills, five thousand feet high, that runs parallel to the river and is home to the villages of Khairi Gaon, Thak, Kumayun Chak, Kot Kindri and others that are referred to as Talla Desh.

The British certainly had an eye for beauty when locating and constructing their rest houses, or homes away from home, and each one of them that I have had the pleasure of visiting is a masterpiece of design and setting. But given a choice, I would unhesitatingly say that Kaladhunga is the finest of them all. Situated away from noisy human habitation, cocooned by verdant trees, with lofty hills at the rear, an emerald river flowing in front and a vista of endless ranges on the horizon, it is endowed with a timeless charm unmatched anywhere in India. Corbett himself was fascinated by the place and described the view from the verandah as the morning sun rose over the distant hills and the mist lifted as one of the most pleasing prospects it was possible to imagine. Straight in front, and across the Sharda, is a wide open valley running deep into Nepal. The hills on either side are densely wooded, and as far as the eye can see, there are no human habitations. Judging from the animal calls that can be heard from the bungalow, there also appears to be an abundant stock of game in the valley.

When we reached Kaladhunga in the afternoon, we found that a lot of work had been done on the rest house to prepare it for our arrival. The old chowkidar and the forest guards told us that thieves came regularly from across the border and indulged not only in poaching, but often also ripped out doors, windows and fittings from the bungalow. These items had recently had to be repaired for our stay. Be that as it may, the staff soon had one of the rooms ready for us while Chotey Lal and the porters occupied the others.

We also found a crowd of about twenty or so people who had come from Thak, Chuka and as far as Kot Kindri to meet the visiting 'Commissioner'. The villagers were led by one Pundit Nand Kishore Misra, a priest at the Purnagiri temple, who belonged to Thak village. Even though I tried my best to convince them that I was not the Commissioner of their division but only out on holiday, they said that I was the first senior officer of my service to ever come to their area and that they were happy to have had my darshan! For my part, I was pleased with their presence, for the villages of Chuka and Thak were the ones we had planned to visit.

Beautiful Kaladhunga Forest Rest House

Around a small log fire in the evening—even though it was April, it was still chilly in the jungle—Vikram related to the gathering stories about how Corbett had gone after the man-eaters and had rid the area of them. We stated that we were fascinated by the accounts and wanted to see for ourselves the places in which the said man-eaters had been killed by Corbett.

There was considerable excitement among the people gathered on hearing our reason for coming. Pundit Nand Kishore Misra spoke first, stating that he had been only ten years of age when the man-eater of Thak was shot in his village more than forty years ago, but the events connected with it were still etched in his memory as if they had occurred yesterday. He said that he could take us to every inch of space through which Carpet Sahib had tracked the man-eater and the rock on which he'd shot it. He added that Jogi Ram of Chuka, who had also come to see us, had actually been with the Sahib when Corbett killed the dreaded man-eater of Chuka. Unfortunately, Dungar Singh, malguzar of Talla Kote, was no longer alive, otherwise we would have been able to see the site where the killer of Talla Desh had been vanquished by Corbett. It is a long way off, but if we so desired, he could call someone from his village to take us there.

We told Pundit Misra that we would not be going as far as Talla Kote, but that we could leave for Chuka after staying a day or two at Kaladhunga. So thus the matter rested, and after a meal of rice, dal and a vegetable curry, shared with the villagers and cooked in a huge dekchi over the wood-fire, we all turned in, with most of the villagers sleeping on the verandah of the rest house.

I awoke once during the night on hearing the belling of a sambar in the hills that rose at the back of the rest house, but otherwise silence reigned over the area.

Most of our visitors left the next morning to make arrangements for our stay at Chuka and beyond, although I tried to explain to them that we would only be staying in the camping tent we had brought with us. Pundit Misra meanwhile organized a fishing party with some of the villagers who did it for a living. A huge tractor's tube was filled with air and allowed to float on the river; the fisherman sat in it with a net to snare the fish. The flow of the river was quite strong and took the angler almost to the edge of the gorge before he manoeuvred it to the side, and carrying the bulky tube, returned to the bungalow. For his efforts, he managed to catch two medium-sized fish that served as our meal for the evening.

Vikram and I made a foray into the hills to exercise our limbs and to see if we could spot any wildlife. We were accompanied by a forester carrying the customary axe and a local resident who ran a tea shop on the road to the gorge. The forester was quite vituperative about the raiders from across the river from Nepal.

'Sir, the Nepali hunters have denuded the forests of everything, particularly the big cats, whose skin, bones and claws command a windfall in China. We try to do what we can to stop them but what are two-three of us compared to the numbers that come poaching. Sometime back the Conservator of Wildlife had come from Lucknow with a raiding party to trap the poachers, but they caught wind of this and did not turn up. What we need is a permanent wildlife chowki here, with well-armed guards to counter the infiltrators. The villagers are also willing to cooperate as they are getting fed up of the raiders and their thefts.'

The tea-stall owner now spoke up and added a bit of drama to our visit.

'Sahib, just a few weeks back, a tiger, coming from the other side of the river, had crossed the road in a leisurely manner very near my tea-shop. We were just getting over this surprise, when a few hours later a group of around seven poachers came by, following the tiger's pug marks. They had powerful rifles with them and looked quite determined in their chase. The tiger had obviously come from Nepal but had disappeared in the forests of the Boom Range where the Devi Ma protected it. We encountered those shikaris again, tired and in a foul mood, as they trudged wearily back to their country.'

'But Sahib,' he added, 'these days we have been hearing the tiger calling a few times in the night and you should be careful when you go into the hills.'

After this, it was a silent group that came back to the rest house.

The next morning, Chotey Lal left with the porters to set up our camp in Chuka. Pundit Nand Kishore Misra and a few of his companions stayed back with us in Kaladhunga, and it is just as well that they did so.

We had retired early that night, so that we would be fresh for the journey ahead. Something woke me, but it was pitch dark when I opened my eyes. Luckily, I had my sturdy pipe lighter with me, and after juggling with it for a while, I was able to light the kerosene lamp on the table. I then looked for the torch near my pillow and had just got a grip on it when I heard what sounded like the most hysterical laughter coming from the back of the bungalow—*heanh, heanh, heanh*!

I nudged Vikram awake and then went to the next room where Misraji and the others were sleeping. The forester awoke and, taking up his faithful axe, opened the rear door and rushed out shouting 'hut, hut', as he banged the axe on the pillars at the back. Hearing this, whatever it was, ran off into the darkness, its hideous calls still echoing.

'Just some jackals, sir,' he announced, 'attracted to the

remains of the food thrown in the bin outside.'

So ended our trauma that day—though not, as we were soon to discover, permanently. This was just the first of our nights in Kaladhunga and Chuka. There was much more to come.

Chuka

After a fitful sleep and an early breakfast, we left for Chuka the next morning. The road from Kaladhunga to Chuka, mostly along the Sharda River, was a pleasant walk of about seven kilometres. The hills and forests which were to one of our sides were showing their first flush of spring, and the air was fresh and alluring. We saw many fish jumping in the flowing water and regretted not having brought our fishing equipment. But the road was also packed with red jungle fowls, pea-fowls and khaleej, and we saw many footmarks of deer and boars, showing us clearly what attracted the poachers to this otherwise peaceful paradise.

Only once along the way did we come across any human inhabitant. It was a young girl pulling two cows many times her size on the road.

Vikram offered her some toffees he always carried and, after some initial hesitation, she shyly accepted and popped them into her mouth.

'Aren't you afraid of walking on this road alone?' Vikram asked her.

Turning her big round eyes on him, she answered,

'No, why should I be?'

'Why, there are all sorts of wild animals—tigers and things,' he said.

'Never seen any tigers; what are they?' she asked.

And as we finished our walk to her village, we asked ourselves, 'Were the stories of the Chuka and Talla Desh man-eaters really true?'

Chuka nestles against heavily-forested hills on one side and the river on the other and, with most of its fields cultivated, shows all the signs of being a thriving agrarian village.

It seemed as if the entire village had come out to greet us as we approached through the lantana bushes on the southern edge of the hamlet. The village Lambardar bade us a warm welcome and took us to his house alongside which our camp tent had been erected. A charpoi was set up next to the tent, and while we were served water and tea to quench our thirst, the topography of the surrounding hills, showing the routes and directions to various places in Talla Desh, was explained to us.

Sem village, which figures so prominently in Corbett's 'Man-eater of Thak', is less than a kilometre north of Chuka, situated on the left side of where the Ladhya River meets with the Sharda. It was here that Corbett and the Ibbotsons had camped when going after that tiger. Thak, on the other hand, was around three kilometres northeast of Chuka, but involved a stiff climb of three thousand feet through a steep ridge of thick jungle and undergrowth that sometimes required one to walk on all fours. A less formidable path along the ridge on the right led to Kot Kindri five kilometres away.

After a light meal of rice and dal, the headman of Chuka, Bishen Singh, who, we discovered, was the son of Kunwar Singh referred to by Corbett, took us to show the place under some trees on the outskirts of the village where Corbett had camped in Chuka. It was then that I mentioned to him something that had been troubling me ever since we had arrived at Chuka. Our tent had been set up almost alongside the village settlements and gave us no privacy from the friendly, if inquisitive, eyes, of the villagers who good-naturedly sat around us all the time.

So as not to hurt any feelings, I said to Bishen Singh, 'Lambardar Sahib, we have come to this place so as to have a Corbett-like experience in the wild. Now that you have shown us the place where he had camped, can we not also set our tent in a similar place? Not too far from the village but still far enough to feel like we are living in the wild. What do you think?'

Bishen Singh was a bit nonplussed at this request and sat down to consult with Pundit Misra and Chotey Lal. Discussion mainly centred on our security, but it was finally concluded that there was now no danger from any wild animal. It was, therefore, decided that our tent would be shifted outside the village near the lantana bushes, but on the condition that Chotey Lal's tent would be set up near ours. It was also suggested that some villagers could camp near the tents but since this meant their sleeping out in the open where there was no shelter, I plainly rejected this offer.

After all of this had been agreed upon, we returned to the village. Our tents were dismantled, much to the amusement of the assembled gathering, and then put up again away from the dwelling.

'Just a few years ago, Sahib, nothing would have persuaded us to let you camp so far from the village. Chuka was known for its tigers and, just four years ago, the nephew of the headman of Sem, a close friend of mine, was killed by a tiger on the riverbed of the Ladhya, when he accidentally ran into it while returning to his hut after smoking a bidi with me. We chased the tiger away and carried my friend all the way to Banbassa, but he died on the way. Since then, luckily, no tiger has been seen anywhere in this area.'

That night a community dinner was hosted by the Lambardar, which was followed, as was the custom, by songs and dances by some of the musically gifted residents. We were then escorted to our tents which now, at night, seemed further from the village than we had envisaged.

Chotey Lal's tent was about twenty yards away and had been put up halfway between our tents and the village.

A petromax lamp was placed near the entrance to our tent to provide some light in the enveloping dark.

So, we changed into our night clothes, got into our sleeping bags, and were tired enough that not even the hard, lumpy floor could prevent us from quickly dozing off.

In the middle of the night, we were suddenly woken by loud chanting of the *Hanuman Chalisa* coming from the direction of Chotey Lal's tent. Quickly emerging from our tent with a torch, we found Chotey Lal squatting outside, dripping wet and singing for all he was worth!

Our camp in Chuka

His tent, unlike ours, was only single-panelled, and the dew had seeped into the top layer to totally drench its occupant inside. We made Chotey Lal change into one of my dry shirts and then rearranged ourselves so he could sleep inside our tent—even so, a portion of his legs still stuck out! And thus, the night passed without further incident.

Early next morning Pundit Misra, Bishen Singh and some of the villagers came with a kettle, cups, biscuits and a kerosene stove to revive us with some hot tea, which to us was a welcome sight. Chotey Lal seemed none the worse after his watery adventure the night before, and while we washed and changed, the camp was soon dismantled by Chotey Lal, who wound his way back to Kaladhunga while we went up to Thak.

࿐

The path from Chuka to Thak begins along a broad track, which runs along the ridge above Chuka for a kilometre or so before it forks into two. While the track that goes straight ahead curves round the ridge to go towards Kot Kindri, the left fork goes literally straight up the hill to Thak without any U-turns to ease the climb. Reading Jim Corbett's accounts of his forays into this area, I am amazed at how many times he—and with him, Ibbotson—climbed up and down this track multiple times in a single day. While the distance is only three kilometres or so, it rises sharply up through dense forests and shrubbery, and in many places, one would have to literally climb on all fours. And all this with a man-eater threatening you every step of the way!

Jogi Ram, a distant relative of Sham Singh who finds mention in Corbett's book, was a youngster at the time of the Chuka man-eater but still knew every inch of the way. It was a surprise how easily he and Pundit Misra negotiated the climb that proved so difficult for us, but we soon came to the place where the Chuka killer had met his end.

While camping at Chuka, Corbett and Ibbotson—a friend of Corbett and District Officer of Kumaon—had tied up a buffalo at the head of a valley to the west of Thak. Soon after, the headman of Thak sent word to them that the buffalo had been killed by a tiger and carried away.

Corbett and Ibbotson reached the scene of the kill at about midday. The tiger, after killing the buffalo and breaking a very strong rope, had picked up the kill and gone straight down into the valley. It soon became apparent that the tiger was making for some definite spot, for he led them for miles through dense undergrowth, down steep banks, through beds of nettle and raspberry bushes, over and under fallen trees, and over great masses of rock until finally he deposited the kill in a small hollow under a box tree shaped like an umbrella. If all went well, there was every reason to hope that the tiger would return to his kill. From the teeth marks on the buffalo's neck, they knew he was the man-eater they were looking for and not just an ordinary tiger.

Corbett was looking for a tree on which to lie in wait, when he noticed that growing on the outer edge of the hollow and leaning away from the hill at an angle of forty-five degrees was a ficus tree. Wrapped round this tree was a trellis, which, ten feet from the ground, made a crude seat on which he could sit.

Immediately below him there was a flat bit of ground about ten feet wide and twenty feet long. From this flat piece of ground the hill fell steeply away. It was overgrown with tall grass and dense patches of brushwood, and beyond it, he could hear a stream running. An ideal place for a tiger to lie up in.

Ibbotson made two men climb up a nearby tree and break branches and leaves to distract the tiger, in case it was nearby. After Corbett climbed the ficus tree, Ibbotson and the rest of the men left for Thak. Corbett sat facing the hill, with the kill in front of him, slightly to his left. Suddenly, on the steep hillside behind him, he heard the sound of a dry twig snapping. Turning his head and looking through the trellis, he saw the tiger standing and looking in the direction of the ficus from a distance of about forty yards. For several minutes he stood still, looking, alternatively, in his direction and then in the direction of the tree that the two men had climbed, until eventually, deciding to come towards Corbett, he started up the steep hillside. The nearer he came to the flat ground the more cautious he became and the closer he kept his belly to the ground. When he was near the top of the bank, he very slowly raised his head, took a long look at the tree that the men had climbed, and satisfied that it was not tenanted, sprang up to the flat ground and proceeded to lie down on the dry leaves under the ficus!

Ficus tree from which Chuka tiger was shot

Corbett leaned towards his left and was able to see the tiger's back and tail but not his head. He knew he had to take the shot to break his back as he lay sleeping, no matter how unsporting or distasteful it might be. The tiger was a man-eater and had killed many people and would kill many more if he let him live. So, he took the shot, and as the tiger started to slide down the hill on his back, Corbett fired a second shot into his chest that effectively killed him.

Somehow, Jogi Ram had unerringly led all of us to this site that was just as Corbett had described. There was the ficus tree, now grown to its full height, among the surrounding trees. There was the trellis, grown almost twenty-five to thirty feet from the ground. And there was the flat land, ten by twenty feet long, from where the hill fell steeply away and was overgrown with dense shrubbery.

The most stunning proof of the place was that, when one stood silent, one could clearly hear the sound of a running stream, just as Corbett had described! Nearly fifty years after the account of the Chuka man-eater's killing had been written, the setting remained as if frozen—only Jim Corbett and the tiger were missing from the scene.

Thak

The village of Thak, situated three thousand feet above Chuka, sits within a bowl formed by a circle of hills. Its well-terraced agricultural fields climb five hundred feet into the surrounding hills. The Chand Rajas who ruled Kumaon before the advent of the Gurkhas had given the lands of Thak to the forefathers of the present holders for their maintenance, and had appointed them hereditary custodians of the Purnagiri temples. Pundit Nand Kishore Misra, who had accompanied us from Kaladhunga, was one such malguzar and owned substantial lands in the village.

In the winter of 1938, when Corbett wrote the story of the man-eater of Thak, this entire area was in considerable turmoil. By an unfortunate coincidence, that summer, the Forest Department had marked the trees around Chuka, Kot Kindri and Kumayun Chak for felling and the contractors brought a large contingent of labourers from the neighbouring villages to perform this task. The labour camps were set up in Chuka and Kumayun Chak, but the reign of the tiger spanned the entire area.

For the residents of Thak, the last couple of years had been a double whammy: first, they had been the unfortunate victims of the Chuka man-eater in the summer of 1937 and then they were subjected to the terror of the Thak killer the following year. The result was that all the residents had abandoned their homes and fled to Chuka for shelter.

Thak, like other villages of Kumaon, had experienced many vicissitudes, but never before in its long history had it been deserted as completely as it was in the winter of 1938 when silence reigned over it. Every single one of the hundred or so inhabitants had fled taking their livestock with them. In fact, so hurried had been the evacuation that many of the doors of the houses were left wide open. On every path in the village, in the courtyards of the houses, and in the dust before all the doors, the tigress's pug marks were visible. The open doorways looked menacing, as if in any of the houses the tigress might still be lurking.

The tigress had killed a man in Thak on November 12 and Corbett had arrived at the deserted village twelve days later. From the headman of Thak, now safely settled in Chuka, he got a graphic account of the events of that day, since the headman himself had barely escaped being a victim of the tigress. Accompanied by his young granddaughter, he had gone to dig some ginger tubers sixty yards from his premises, when his wife, who was husking rice in the courtyard of his house, alerted him to the presence of a red animal at the upper end of the field. The headman acted with alacrity, and grabbing the child's hand, ran back to the safety of his dwelling.

Half an hour later, three hundred yards from the headman's house, the tigress killed a man cutting leaves from a tree.

A fortnight later, it was in this spectral setting of an abandoned village that Corbett would have a brush with the occult that he would never be able to explain.

He had been sitting in a machan twenty yards above a dead buffalo that had been tied up earlier. The buffalo had been killed by the tigress, and Corbett was hoping that the man-eater would return for the rest of it. He had sent his men back to camp earlier, refusing their request to be permitted to stay the night in one of the houses in Thak, knowing that this would be too dangerous. They went, huddled close to each other for safety, as Corbett counted to ensure that each and every one of them had indeed left. Then an eerie silence descended on the village.

There was still sufficient daylight to shoot by when the moon—just a day short of the full—rose over the Nepal hills behind him, flooding the hillside with its brilliant light. The light was so bright that he was able to see a sambhar and her young one feeding in a field of wheat a hundred and fifty yards away. The moon had been up for two hours and the sambhar had approached to within fifty yards of his tree, when a kakkar started barking on the hill just above the village. The kakkar had been barking for some minutes when suddenly a scream—*ar-ar-arr*, dying away on a long-drawn-out note—came from the direction of the village.

So surprised was Corbett that he involuntarily stood up with the intention of slipping down from the machan and rushing to the village, thinking that the man-eater had attacked one of his men. Then he recalled seeing them off safely on their way back to camp.

Corbett stated that the scream had sounded to him like the despairing cry of a human being in mortal agony, although reason made him question how such a sound could come from a deserted village. It was not a thing of his imagination, for the kakkar had heard it and abruptly stopped barking, and the sambhar had also dashed away across the fields closely followed by her young one.

The screams were not repeated, and at daybreak Corbett's men returned to bring him down from the machan. When he returned to Chuka, he questioned the headman again about the kill at Thak on the 12th of the month, when he had so narrowly escaped falling victim to the man-eater.

The headman told him in great detail how he had gone to his fields to dig ginger, taking his grandchild with him, and how on hearing his wife calling he had taken hold of the child's hand and ran back to the house—where his wife told him off for not keeping his ears open and thereby endangering his own and the child's lives—and how a few minutes later the tigress had killed a man who was cutting leaves from a tree in a field above his house. When Corbett asked how he knew the man had been killed, the headman replied, 'Because I had heard him.' In reply to further questions, he explained that the man had not called for help but had cried out; and when asked if he had cried out once, the headman clarified that the dead man cried out three times. Then the headman imitated the man's cry. It was the same sound, though slightly modified, as the screams that Corbett had heard from his machan the previous night.

Corbett then told him about what he had heard and asked him if it was possible for anyone to have arrived at the village accidentally and his answer was an emphatic no. Corbett then dismissively stated that it would be best to assume that neither the kakkar, nor the sambar, nor he had heard those very real screams—the screams of a human being in mortal agony.

Having read these accounts of Corbett in Thak, we asked Pundit Misra whether he had heard the stories about the screams, and if so, how he explained them. Pundit Misra confirmed that the story of the strange cries of a person in extreme agony was very real and that every person in Thak was familiar with them. As for their explanation, he paused for a long time and then said,

'Sahib, in these far-off villages of the Kumaon, strange things are known to happen. Only persons who are acutely attuned to the supernatural can experience them. Corbett Sahib was one such person who had witnessed so much suffering and deaths in these hills that he had become sensitive to these occurrences. You remember how he saw the lights in the Sharda Gorge—which only appear to the specially blessed—or what happened to him at the Phungarh bungalow near Champawat about which he never spoke to anyone. Perhaps even here, what he heard were the despairing cries of a person in mortal terror seeking succour from certain death or justice for an unnatural demise.'

'Dayanand, the man who was killed,' he continued, 'was eagerly looking forward to the sacred thread ceremony of his four-year-old son, Umed Chand, and had been avidly collecting customary items and clothes for the same. His dying cries were a heart-rending protest at the injustice of it all and maybe the vibrations lay frozen in the air till they were picked up by Corbett Sahib.'

'This is the closest to an explanation that I can offer,' he sadly concluded.

'But come, sir, let me show you around the other places mentioned in his description of Thak.'

So, accompanied by a sizable crowd from the village, we were led on an expedition to Thak's various sites.

As you approach Thak, the distinguishing feature of the village is a giant mango tree, from the roots of which issues a cold spring of clear water that is gathered in a masonry trough. After the steep climb up from Chuka, this water, proffered to us in earthenware cups by the villagers, tasted exceedingly sweet. From the trough the water seeps into the surrounding ground, which is slushy and covered by green grass. In Corbett's story, this was the place where he found the pug marks of the tigress superimposed on his own.

After resting under the mango tree for some time, we climbed the hill above Thak, from where we got a bird's-eye view of the terraced fields, and of the Ladhya River far below, just before it joins the Sharda.

Tiwari, the present headman, pointed out where his father, the headman in Corbett's story, had barely escaped becoming a victim of the tigress, having been alerted to its presence in the nick of time by his wife. The tree from which the last victim, Dayanand, had been dragged down by the tigress stood on the hill three hundred yards away. His now fifty-year-old son, Umed Chand, wistfully stood by this stunted chilly tree, which grew at an angle from the terraced field, and, as Vikram put it, was now almost black 'with shame'.

Our tour of Thak over, we now went down the valley to see the site where the man-eater was finally shot.

As he had gone down the path that joined the ridge running down to Chuka, Corbett had heard the tigress calling on his left. She was a little above and to the left of Kumayun Chak and a few hundred yards below the Kot Kindri ridge on which the men were working. The day was drawing to a close and Corbett calculated that he had roughly half an hour's daylight in hand. There were four men with Corbett and two goats, and their destination was still at quite a distance. The tigress was a mile away and the intervening ground was densely wooded, strewn with boulders and cut up by a number of deep nullahs, but she could cover the distance well within the half-hour if she wanted to.

Corbett was in a serious dilemma—one that could affect the lives of all who were with him. The question that had to be decided was whether or not to call the tigress. If he called and she came while there was still daylight, he would have a shot and all could be well. On the other hand, if she came and was not shot, some of them would surely not live to reach camp, which was still two miles away through thick jungle. So, selecting a suitable rock to sit on, and with his four men and two goats positioned behind the rock, Corbett started calling to the tigress.

It took us a while to find the site where the final act had been actually played out.

Again, closely following the directions he provided in his book, we went over the land foot by foot as if participating in a treasure hunt. And what a treasure hunt it was! Starting from the ridge that runs down to Chuka, a quarter of a mile from Thak, one would have to get to a spot where the ridge was only a few feet wide and from there a view would be obtained of the two great ravines that ran down to the Ladhya River. The entire area was heavily wooded and thick-set shrubs covered the few remaining open patches. Four hundred yards down the ridge, the path ran for fifty yards across a relatively flat patch of ground. This rectangular piece of land was forty yards wide and eighty yards long and ended in a more or less perpendicular rock face.

The path coming from Thak crossed this ground at its southern or shorter end and, going down the centre, exited the rectangle on its long or east side. Corbett then identifies the one critical item in the entire setting—a solitary rock at the far side of the flat ground where the path, skirting this big rock, dropped steeply and continued in a series of hairpin bends down to the next bend.

The rock was about four feet high and, projecting out of it on the nearer side, was a narrow ledge on which, sitting sideways, Corbett could face the direction from which the tigress would be coming. Behind and below him were huddled the four men and the two goats, frozen into silence at the approaching menace. The last two calls from the tigress and Corbett overlapped with each other. Then, stepping out into the open, she looked into his eyes and stopped dead. It was in this position that Corbett's bullets hit her and she died with her nose against the rock.

Corbett's description of the rectangular piece of open ground, with a four-foot-high rock on its far right and a narrow ledge running across its upper face, tallied exactly with what we found so many years later. We reached the conclusion that he had, either then or perhaps some time later, revisited the place to make detailed notes to correspond with actual reality. Vikram climbed on to the ledge and had his photograph taken—sitting just as Corbett must have sat when he shot the Thak man-eater.

Vikram posing on the rock from where the Thak man-eater was shot

It was now getting late in the evening and we had a long way to go—first, down to Chuka, and then to Kaladhunga. Pundit Misra then suggested that we take a shortcut that would circumvent Chuka and bring us closer to our destination. This was a path known as Suwadh Garh ka Nallah, which descended through a truly dense forest and which used to be one of the most dangerous places in the olden days.

The track here was even more steep than the direct path to Chuka and was full of closely compacted and overgrown shrubbery and one had to carefully watch one's footing. A stream coming from the hills flowed over the rocks making them slippery, thus making our trek even more perilous.

Pundit Misra proclaimed, much to our discomfort,

'Sahib, many people had been killed here in the days of the Chuka and Thak tigers; in those far-off days, few dared to use this route. Now, of course, there is talk of a new road being built here; the Purnagiri Temple authorities are also considering the issue.'

Listening to such reassurances, I was jumping from one rock to another when I slipped on the wet moss and landed flat on my back in a shallow pool. The gun I was holding had even worse luck: it was found with difficulty and was dripping with mud and water.

After the others had stopped smirking at my misfortune, we stopped to rest. I also had to find a way to dry my clothes. I borrowed a bidi from Pundit Misra and the discussion wound round to how craftily Corbett had called up the man-eater from the rock. Then, to the amusement of the others, and the horror of Vikram, I tried to imitate what I imagined was a mating call of a tiger!

'Dad,' Vikram asked earnestly, 'what are you trying to do in this ghastly and dangerous place?'

'Aw, come on Vikram, don't be a skit; as a shikari of repute I was only trying to summon a tiger to meet us, but sadly, this place is bereft of them.'

Of course, I had very little knowledge of tigers' calls and even less ability to copy them, so the matter ended there.

It was, however, now getting quite late as well as a trifle gloomy as we picked ourselves up from that pool in Suwadh Garh ka Nallah. It was a silent and bedraggled group that made its way back to the rest house in Kaladhunga in semi-darkness. However, at Kaladhunga, Chotey Lal and the villagers had a welcome and roaring log fire going. With my clothes drying and with a hearty dinner of rice and dal under our belt, our mood soon lifted.

The next morning, we wound up our camp, and as the porters carried off our luggage to Baramdeo, we bid farewell to Pundit Misra and the affectionate villagers from Talla Desh, promising them that we would come again as soon as opportunity presented itself. It had been a most informative and adventurous foray into the home of the man-eaters of eastern Kumaon but, as always, there was still a sting in the tail.

On the way back to the Sharda Gorge, we stopped at a tea dhaba on the picturesque forest road. I asked the owner whether he had heard of the tiger that had come from Nepal.

A tea dhaba on the picturesque forest road

'No Sahib,' he replied. 'We had heard that the tiger had crossed the river and returned to his home, and I was also told that the Nepali police and forest officials had arrested some of the poachers who were after it and were hot on the trail of others. But just the other day, as some people from Thak were going to Tanakpur for monthly provisions, they came across a menacing tiger in their path. Luckily, there were quite a few of them, and probably seeing their numbers, the tiger decided it was best to let them go.'

'Where was this?' I asked.

'In the Suwadh Garh Nallah, Sahib,' he replied.

I tried not to look at Vikram's piercing and accusing glare!

The Mohan Man-Eater

As one drives north along National Highway 121, around twenty-one kilometres from Ramnagar, one comes to the township of Mohan, where the road divides into two—the northern branch goes to Marchula and the right hand or eastern fork goes to Naini Tal. At this junction, and slightly above Mohan township, is located the Mohan Forest rest house. The rest house commands glorious views of the river Kosi, which flows in front of it, and the hills, which, beyond the rocky stream, rise to above 4,000 feet. The Forest Range Office is behind and to the side of the bungalow, which is otherwise surrounded by rich forest going along the road that runs past it.

My wife and I were guests of the forest department and were regaled with stories of the wildlife that lived around the place and which were often seen from the wide verandah of the artistically constructed building. Apart from many species of the deer family that one could hear at night, herds of elephant were also regular visitors to the Kosi River, to which they came to quench their thirst and to wallow and bathe. The Corbett National Park was nearby and we heard stories of leopards and tigers frequently being spotted along the highway.

One morning, soon after we came to Mohan, an elderly forester, Ram Singh, who belonged to Mohan village, pointed to a small white structure we could see high up on the ridge in the foreground and said, 'Sir, that is the forester's hut in which Corbett Sahib had stayed when he was hunting the Man-Eater of Mohan which had terrorized this area many years ago. The man-eater used to traverse the river right up to Gargia and had led to a virtual curfew being imposed in these parts. But he made the hut up on that ridge, where many people were killed and eaten, his home. The village on the ridge is known as Kartkanoula (now Kaath ki Nav, or the wooden boat), and if you are interested, we can go there.'

My wife quickly fished out our copy of the *Man-Eaters of Kumaon* and we read all we could on the Mohan Man-Eater. Fortified with this knowledge, we set off for Kaath ki Nav the next day.

During Corbett's days, as is described in his book, one had to make the practically vertical climb up the ridge to Kaath ki Nav on foot. Now, however, there is a motorable road to Kaath ki Nav. You go up the NH 121, take the left where the road forks at Mohan Chowk—the one marked for Marchula—and then take a right about 10 kilometres up the road at Chimthakhal. This path, coming up north of the Kaat ki Nav ridge, takes you to the village centre.

We sat down to have tea at the local dhaba while Ram Singh explained to the villagers our interest in the man-eater.

The story was set so far back in time that there were few alive who had actually witnessed the events though, of course, all had heard of the tiger's thrall over the area, not least from tourists like us who came to visit the place. Still, there were some, and when prodded on by Ram Singh, the village Pradhan went and fetched a distant relative who coincidentally was one of the oldest residents of Kaath ki Nav.

Stooping slightly over his walking stick, wearing thick glasses and with patches strategically stitched on to his jacket, this relative was only a young lad when the events related in Corbett's book had taken place. Accompanied by many of the villagers, we were taken to the forester's hut where Corbett had stayed. The old hut was a long wooden structure converted into one hall where earlier there had been three rooms.

The ridge, which overlooks Kosi and Mohan, is at this point about fifty yards long. The hut is on its south end and the village of Kaath ki Nav is to the north. The hut stands on a little knoll some twenty yards to the left of the road that winds down the face of the hill to Chaknakl on the Ramganga River. This portion of the road between Kaath ki Nav and Chaknakl, some eight kilometres long, traverses through dense forest and scrub jungle. It was considered to be very dangerous in the days of the man-eater—most of the kills occurred along this area.

While we were being told all this by the Pradhan's relative, a sudden and very powerful squall suddenly hit the ridge and it was with great difficulty—holding on to each other and the creaking wooden railing leading up to the structure—that we managed to open the door of the hut and somehow tumble inside. The villagers also crawled in with us and thus escaped the gale and the sharp rain that followed. But this gave us the chance, sitting hunched on the ledge of the hut, to continue to listen to the story of the man-eater.

'Sahib', the relative said, 'in those far-off days one had never heard of a tiger becoming so vicious as to actually eat human beings. Yes, of course, we had thick forests all around with plenty of wild animals in them, but, apart from the destruction of our crops, we had no complaints against the jungle dwellers.'

'Then, one day,' he continued, 'as a group of women were out cutting grass on the hillside, a tiger suddenly appeared in their midst—and in the confusion that followed, an elderly woman tripped, rolled down the steep slope and over the cliff. The tiger, alarmed by the screams of the women, vanished as mysteriously as he had appeared. When the women had recovered from their fright, they searched for their companion and found her lying on a ledge along the cliff, badly injured. After discussion, it was decided to fetch some men from the village to bring her up. While the rest of the women went back, one brave sixteen-year-old girl agreed to stay back with the injured woman.'

He paused as if gathering his thoughts and then said,

'Sahib, when the rescue party came, they found the injured woman lying on the ledge in a swoon, and where the girl had been, there were splashes of blood, broken bangles and a few bits of bone. When the old woman recovered her senses she narrated how, sometime after the rest of the women had gone, the tiger returned and coming down the narrow ledge, killed and carried the girl away.

'That brave young girl was my grandmother's cousin

sister and was known as much for her good looks as for her helpful nature. Who else would have gone down a cliff to sit with an injured old woman—no relative of hers—knowing fully well that there was a fierce tiger on the prowl? She was betrothed to a rich malguzar's son from Baital Ghat and her demise in this cruel and unnecessary manner cast a pall of gloom over the whole village.

'She was the first known victim of the tiger that went on to acquire the name of the Mohan Man-eater, and who, for some reason, liked this ridge of Kaath ki Nav where you are now sitting. Most nights, it used to come to the road in front of this hut. It would growl menacingly and leave scratch marks on the doors of the huts as it tried to gain access to the terrified occupants inside, shouting and banging on utensils and everything else they could lay their hands on to scare it away. Sir, it was in this manner that we spent our lives till Corbett Sahib came and rid us of the beast.'

By then, the rain and squalls had ended and we walked out to the sweet-smelling fragrance of a forest washed of its dust and sooty haze. We slowly walked down the pretty but erstwhile 'road of dread' and some distance away were shown the overhanging rock over the road. Here Corbett had been saved from becoming a victim of the man-eater by his sixth-sense warning him of impending danger.

He was returning at sunset and was about thirty yards from the overhanging rock when he felt he was in danger, and that the danger that threatened him was close to the rock in front of him. With only half an hour of daylight left, and the best part of a mile still to go, it would have been madness to have left the road. So, slipping off the safety catch and putting the rifle on his shoulder, he started to pass the rock.

The road here was about eight feet wide, and going to the extreme outer edge, he started walking like a crab, feeling each step with his feet. Progress was slow and difficult, but as he drew level with the overhanging rock and began to pass it, hope rose in him that the tiger would remain where it was until he reached that part of the road from which the flat bit of ground above the rock, on which the tiger was lying, would be clearly visible, thereby giving him a shot.

The tiger, however, having failed to catch him off his guard, was not interested in taking any more chances. Corbett had just got clear of the rock when the tiger let out a low growl from above him, and a little later, first a kakkar went off barking to the right, and then two sambar hind started belling near the crest of the triangular hill.

The tiger had got away with its skin intact, but, for that matter, so had Corbett!

We were now on the hill overlooking Mohan, and the Pradhan's relative was clearly tired from the exertion as, frankly, were we. He showed us the steep ridge that Corbett had gone down while tracking the buffalo that had been the last kill of the tiger. Somewhere down there, the reign of the Mohan Man-Eater had finally ended. As we made our weary way back to Kaath ki Nav, we couldn't help but wonder at the stamina of the man who had trudged up and down these ravines and almost vertical hillsides, loaded down with a heavy rifle, with the sole aim of freeing the villagers from a dreaded scourge.

But sad as we were for the victims of the man-eater, we couldn't help also feeling sorry for the tiger that was shot while sleeping without being given a chance to defend itself. I know this sounds silly especially so many years after the event, but our feelings were given a thrust with something that the Pradhan showed us as we were leaving Kaath ki Nav.

Apparently when Corbett was skinning the dead tiger, he drew from its left leg twenty-five or thirty porcupine quills, some as long as five inches, that had lodged themselves under its skin and caused its left leg to become infected, making it moan in pain every time it tried to walk.

The villagers had kept some of these porcupine quills as mementos but they only served to sadden us further.

Ranthambore

'Tigers? What tigers?' said Vikram, in a semi-serious voice. 'Yes, we've seen them in zoos and I have even personally handled them as cubs. But seeing them in the wild? No, never; think of all the places we've been to and the miles we've driven in Pilibhit, Naini Tal, Lakhimpur Kheri and elsewhere. I don't think they are in the wild any more except, perhaps, in Siberia. Everywhere else, they've all been killed off. I think I will do a story on them someday.'

My wife echoed this sentiment.

'The times you saw tigers in the jungle were years ago and I must have by now driven hundreds of kilometres in our beautiful forests. But apart from stray deer and plenty of monkeys, have seen not even a tail of our famous carnivore, I am now sadly led to conclude, as Jim Corbett had done way back in the 1940s, that 'a tiger is a large-hearted gentleman with boundless courage and that when he is exterminated—as exterminated he will be unless public opinion rallies to his support—India will be the poorer, having lost the finest of her fauna.'

I heard all this with great trepidation, as I tended to

agree with the broad force of their argument. The tiger, who once roamed free in all the jungles of India, was now confined to a handful of sanctuaries and even there, was not free from poaching.

As if to echo this point, Vikram said, 'Look what's happened in Panna, in Rewa and in Sariska, where tigers have been wiped out despite being in so-called sanctuaries. Look at what's happening virtually every other day even in your blessed Corbett Park!

'What a pity we didn't grant tigers the status of citizens in our Constitution. They don't have a vote, so they don't really matter. Shoot them, kill them, exterminate them and it still won't be genocide. How many tigers are left in the wild in all? 1,400? 1,500? Don't worry; soon there will be none, and then Jim Corbett's dire prediction will have come true.'

To try and steer this depressing conversation towards something more positive, I mentioned that I had met the rather dynamic Minister of Tourism of Rajasthan that week and she had invited me to visit the Ranthambore Fort to see how it could be added to our national tourism circuit. I asked my family if they would be interested in coming along with me. The state government would arrange for our stay at Jogi Mahal, within the Ranthambore Park. We would have a grandstand view of the wildlife in the area as Jogi Mahal was in the heart of the sanctuary and just 500 metres from the famous fortress.

My daughter, Sanyukta, could not come as she had her school exams and so went to her grandparents', but my wife and Vikram were eager to come with me. We sent our Gypsy ahead to Jogi Mahal and travelled to Sawai Madhopur by train. We reached at about 10:30 p.m. Jogi Mahal is eleven kilometres from the railway station and it was, therefore, quite late at night when we checked in at the quaint but beautiful red-sandstone bungalow set on the edge of the Padam Talao, the largest of the many lakes located in the park.

The chowkidar of the place met us and showed us to our two rooms, which faced each other, separated by a quadrangle of about forty yards. On one side of this open square was a gigantic banyan tree—considered to be India's second largest—whose branches covered the square and almost touched the building. Vikram was to stay in one room and we in the other. A kerosene lantern was placed in the rooms to provide a meagre light. Each room had a rickety door with four glass panes, through which one could look outside, and could be shut by a weak overhead latch.

Before leaving, the chowkidar said to us,

'Sir, please don't forget that you are in the middle of a forest full of wild animals. They roam freely here. That banyan tree outside provides comfort and shade to many, and a tiger regularly sleeps under it. So, under no circumstances should you go out into the courtyard and put your life in danger. The forest staff will come in the morning to show you around.'

With those words of warning ringing in our ears, we closed the door, and putting out the kerosene lamp, soon fell asleep.

We were awakened, an hour or so later, by relentless pounding on our door. I am a deep sleeper and it took some time before my wife could shake me awake. As she sat up in bed, I took my small bedside torch and went to the door. Opening it, I found a white-faced Vikram, now clutching on to my arm and saying,

'Dad, can I come in and sleep with you people?'

Of course he could, and as he stumbled into the room, I swung the light from my torch once round the quadrangle and then, shutting the door, came back to bed that now had a slightly tremulous Vikram lying next to me.

Next morning, as we sat on the gorgeous verandah overlooking the Padam Talao and waited for our morning tea, Vikram narrated his harrowing experience from the night before.

'After the chowkidar left, I changed into my night clothes, put out the light and was soon asleep. I was awakened by gentle but persistent knocking on the glass pane of the door. I could hear a faint sound, as if someone was crying. Thinking it was your way of playing a prank and scaring me, I sleepily shouted,

'Dad, I am sleeping; go away, stop trying to scare me.'

'The knocking stopped for a while, but then it became louder. This time, there was also a slight wailing sound. Still convinced that it was you, I covered my head with my sleeping bag shouting at you to go away.

'But the knocking wouldn't stop, and it was accompanied by that mysterious crying sound. This now both annoyed and puzzled me, so, getting out of bed, I slowly crept to the door, thinking to myself that I would catch you in the act. But the knocking suddenly stopped and just as I was turning around to go back to the bed, it started again and this time with renewed vigour as if whoever it was on the other side would tear down the door itself.'

'Could it be some wild animal? Perhaps even the tiger?' I thought.

'I stood on tiptoe to peep outside the door to see who it was—but there was no one there.

'The waxing moon was throwing a pale ghostly light on the courtyard, and it was completely bare and bereft of anybody.

'Then the thought struck me and I felt as though I had found the solution. It was a sudden squall that was responsible both for the knocking on the door and the wailing sound. But as the knocking resumed with greater ferocity, I looked at the branches of the banyan tree, and not a leaf was stirring.

'I also heard what I now thought was low hysterical laughter, but I had had enough.

'So, opening the door, I ran across the empty quadrangle to wake you while the door behind me shut with a loud creaking sound.'

The renovated courtyard and door of Jogi Mahal

We were just pondering over what Vikram had told us when the chowkidar came with his ghunghat-covered wife bearing a tray with tea.

We asked Vikram to again narrate what he had experienced, and when he finished, we saw the chowkidar and his wife exchange a long look. He gave a low cough and muttered,

'Sahib, Baba should not have slept in that room alone. Sometimes strange things are known to happen in this old building. Tonight we will lay out your beds on this verandah.'

And that, as the saying goes, was that.

After getting ready we got into the Gypsy, accompanied by two forest guards, and set off on a round of the park. Vikram, with his camera, was seated on the stepney with his legs tucked inside the vehicle. My wife and I were crammed into the front seat next to the driver.

It was early in the morning and we were getting our fill of the sweet smells of winter: deciduous forests and open, grassy meadows. We saw a lot of grey partridges and peafowl pecking alongside the road and quite a few variety of deer including chital, nilgai and sambar.

Suddenly one of the forest guards said 'Sher' and the Gypsy shuddered to a halt. There, in front of us on the road, was the King of the Jungle himself, walking towards us with not a care in the world!

How do you describe a moment you have longed for all your life? My family had driven for miles through forests big and small, in all kinds of weather—hot, icy cold, rainy and dry—and had not been favoured by the sight of so much as the tip of a tiger's tail. Even I had only seen it from machans or during chance encounters. Yet, here it was, in all its majesty, calmly walking as if to say, *Here, you wanted to see me? So, see me, as I show myself—totally unafraid of you.*

The tiger passed no more than a foot alongside the Gypsy and then turned behind it to pass the stepney. All this while Vikram had been continuously taking photos of it. Coming to the back of the Gypsy, the tiger paused. It was at touching distance from Vikram, but it paused. One of its paws was raised, as he looked quizzically up at my son. The forest guard quietly said, 'Baba, aap zor se hilo mat, dheere se andar aajao. Don't make any sudden movements, slowly come inside.'

Luckily Vikram followed his advice and slowly backed into the rear seat! The tiger saw him do this and left as if saying to himself, *So kid, you've seen me at close quarters. Be careful of a swipe of my paw!*

And so ended our first encounter with a tiger in its natural habitat.

After an early lunch, while the family rested, I went up to see the Ranthambore Fortress with the Tourism officials who had come from Jaipur.

If the Park is famous today for its tigers and wildlife, the Fort that dominates it and that gives it its name has the imprint of history written all over it. Constructed in the mid-10th century and improved on for a few centuries after, it was variously occupied by the famous of India's annals—the Chauhans, the Sultans of Delhi including Mohammad Ghori, Iltutmish, Balban and Alauddin Khilji, Sultan Bahadur Shah of Gujarat and the Mughal Emperor, Akbar the Great.

The fortress was also under the rule of various kings of Mewar: Rana Hamir Singh, Rana Kumbha and Rana Sangha.

The fortress had passed to the Kushwaha Maharajas of Jaipur in the 17th century, and it remained a part of Jaipur State. The area surrounding the fortress had been a hunting ground for the Maharajas of Jaipur, till the state acceded to India and became a part of Rajasthan in 1950.

Around the fortress was the Ranthambhore Park, which was established as the Sawai Madhopur Game Sanctuary in 1955 and declared to be one of the Project Tiger reserves in 1973. It became a National Park in 1980 and its territory was expanded to include the adjoining Keladevi and Sawai Mansingh Sanctuaries to ultimately cover an area of 1,334 sq. km.

Returning from the fortress, the Park officials took us for a ride to see the Raj Bagh ruins near Jogi Mahal. Mostly submerged now, these ancient stone structures comprised palace outhouses, pillars, arches, domes and courtyards that had once housed the rulers who inhabited the place.

It was an eerie scene and just as we were imagining what it would be like to live in such a ghostly place, we saw a young tigress emerge from the side and go splashing in the water towards the ruins. No sooner had she done so when a bigger tiger, who had obviously been watching from the courtyard, came bounding out, and with a huge roar, attacked the newcomer. For a full minute or two, and just fifty yards away from where we were watching spellbound, the two tigers savagely attacked each other, all the while emitting the most frightful roars. Then the bigger tiger gave a huge punch and knocked her adversary into the water. For a while the younger one stayed where she lay, staring and growling at her opponent, who stood menacingly over her, then quietly got up and slunk away to the side.

The forest staff who were with us, and totally familiar with the identities of the tigers, told us,

'Sahib, these were mother and daughter. The older tigress was Noor and the younger one her daughter from a previous litter who was obviously wanting to come home to her. But Noor has a new litter among the ruins and is guarding them even from her own grown-up daughter.'

Be as it may, we had had a ringside view of two tigers fighting—a sight one does not ordinarily get to witness anywhere.

But a final surprise was waiting for us at Jogi Mahal.

We had dinner and then lay down on the beds that had been arranged in the front verandah overlooking the Padam Talao. It was a beautiful setting—surrounded on three sides by forest with the lake shimmering in front. The moon, now three-quarters full, lit the entire area with a white, translucent glow and we went to sleep lulled by the sounds of the night jars, the chirruping insects and the croaking of frogs.

Sometime during the night we were awakened by the roaring of a tiger. It was coming from behind the building where the banyan tree was. His call was answered by another tiger slightly further away. For a while this symphony went on, call answered by call, and all the while the tiger that seemed to be nearer to us seemed to be coming closer and closer. We were sleeping out in the open and every time it roared it was as if he was there, amongst us.

I was just beginning to wonder if a tiger would be able to jump onto the verandah where we were, when he came to the platform on the ground floor, lay down there, just below us and continued his dialogue with the other tiger.

We could hear his breathing and the huge intake of air every time he inhaled to let out his roar.

All this while we had gone deeper into our sleeping bags and frozen into absolute silence so as not to attract his attention.

Not so our doughty chowkidar of Jogi Mahal—banging his lathi on the floor of the house, he kept shooing away the tiger as if it were a dog or a cat. And sure enough, we heard the King of the Jungle give one protesting *wrufh* as he went back to the folds of the wild.

What a day it had been!

The next morning as the chowkidar brought us our tea, I asked him about the tiger that had been roaring and about its coming to rest in the verandah below us.

'Weren't you afraid of him? What if he'd barged into your room? And what if he'd climbed up the stairs to come up here? There was only a door separating him from us.'

The chowkidar gave a knowing smile.

'Sahib, he comes here almost every other day. Normally the banyan tree at the back is where he rests, but this is the mating season and he was roaring to his mate to join him. And no, Sahib, he is used to my shouts and would not dare ignore my scolding.'

We tried to look for his pug marks around the bungalow but were too inexperienced to recognize them. We handsomely rewarded the chowkidar and his wife for looking after us and were soon ready to depart.

It was our last day in Ranthambore and it was a nostalgic group that went for a last ride through the Park.

The day was like any other mild winter day in Rajasthan. However, for us, the crisp morning provided the perfect ambience for enjoying the undulating landscape of brown grasslands, interspersed with green forests of acacia, babul, neem, banyan and peepul. The towering fortress on the horizon was like a surrealist painting done by a giant hand on the canvas of the sky. And by then, we had seen a surfeit of wildlife, enough to last us for a long while.

It was in this mood that we came to a small windswept plateau that had an old three-arched rectangular structure on it. From one side of it we suddenly saw a tiger climb up, and standing in all its majesty, give a long hard stare up the slope.

Following his gaze, we saw four chital grazing on the gentle ridge. They were hidden from the tiger's view by a knoll on the hillside and the bushes that covered it. The tiger, however, had seen or heard them and quietly went towards the deer, crawling on its belly. It was an amazing sight—seeing the tiger silently stalking his prey. Just as we thought he was within range of the deer, a peafowl hidden in the bushes flew off in alarm, letting out its loud *meowr, meowr* warning cry. The chital were off in the twinkling of an eye. The tiger slowly sat down, licked its front paw and looking at us, it seemed to clearly say that it was all a part of the game!

So ended our sojourn in that wonderful place and now no one could say we hadn't had our fill of tigers. As we drove back to Delhi with a brief stopover in Jaipur, my mind was full of thoughts of how we could greatly multiply this species and add to the richness of our country's tapestry.

Yes, we had since childhood been brought up on the thrilling stories of the jungles of Kumaon and Garhwal, and of the man-eaters—tigers and leopards—who had terrorized the people living there in the early nineties, written in the beautiful prose of Jim Corbett and his sister Maggie. But there were hardly any tales of tigers/tigresses living among humans as veritable pets, as grown-up mammals leading ordinary lives among people.

It was then that I heard of the very warm, poignant and, in the end, somewhat sad story of a real tigress, Khairi, living as a pet in the jungles of the Similipal forest reserves in Orissa, and of the great forester who looked after her, Saroj Raj Choudhury.

So, here is the tale of Khairi and of Saroj Raj Choudhury who literally lived and died with her.

Khairi

The Similipal Forest Reserve is deep inside Orissa (now Odisha), in the Mayurbhanj district. In 1974, which is when this story begins, Saroj Raj Choudhury was posted as Field Director of the Tiger Reserve, headquartered at Jashipur.

In October 1974, a group of twelve Khadias, a local tribe of the district, were gathering honey from beehives when, along the river Khairi, they suddenly came across a tigress with three cubs. The villagers made considerable noise with their implements, and the somewhat startled mother disappeared into the thick bushes of the forest and into a cave with two of her cubs. The third cub was weak, and in a completely rundown condition, looking almost skeletal, and was unable to follow its mother. Two of the Khadias rushed to catch the cub and quickly wrapped her in a cloth. So sudden was her capture that the poor thing was struck dumb and made no attempt to call its mother.

The next morning, with the cloth-covered cub secure in their resin basket, they brought it, chained and tied with ropes, to the forest rest house where the Director was staying. Saroj Raj Choudhury lifted the cub from the basket, removed the chain and ropes, and gently hugged the cub while speaking to it softly. The cub responded to this by purring gently. When Saroj handed her over to his cousin, Nihar Nalini, she also hugged the cub and gently stroked its back. The cub responded to this by licking Nihar all over.

And thus began the relationship between Khairi, who was named after the river where she was found, and her newfound foster parents—a relationship that lasted for over six years. Khairi weighed only 6.2 kg when she arrived, but over the next few months, she became a full-grown adult, weighing nearly 200 kg—a large female of the big Similipal tiger race. But she was always loving and trusting of her adopted family and of the animals living there.

The very next day after her adoption, the cub made friends with Blackie, their female pet dog, and a few weeks later, with Blackie's pup, Bagha, who, as he grew older, became her constant companion. Then there was Bhaina, the male blind and striped hyena who was often a bully to Khairi, but whom she good-naturedly tolerated. Jambo, the male bear cub, was brought to the family in January 1979 when he was hardly two weeks old. He was the naughtiest of the lot and was Khairi's last companion before she passed away.

Khairi went with Saroj and Nihar to all the camps they went to in and around Similipal, and was lost only once when they camped at Kairakacha camp, in the interior of the core area of the tiger reserve, for the first time. Khairi used to go around the camp in the morning for her daily prowl, but this was a new area that she had not visited before.

She apparently began to trail a barking deer and was missing the whole morning. She had not returned till late that night even though Saroj and Nihar searched for her for miles around Kairakacha. Midnight passed and both the parents started despairing, when three jeeps bearing the Minister of Tourism and his staff drove into the camp. Accompanying the minister was one of the project officers of the reserve. They were all very sorry to hear of the missing Khairi but assured Saroj that she would soon be found.

And so she was: half an hour later one of the jeeps came back with the welcome news that Khairi had been located! She had walked out onto the road where the jeeps were travelling. She'd heard their sounds and probably hoped that her parents would be in them! The vehicles stopped on seeing her and while one was sent back to call Saroj and Nihar, the occupants of the other two jeeps got down—a bit scared to be sure—to be smelled and greeted by the tigress. Not seeing her foster parents there, Khairi went back into the thick jungle.

Soon after, Saroj and Nihar came to the site, and Nihar loudly called out to Khairi, 'Khairi, Khairi, aaja, aaja!'

On hearing her beloved mother's call, the tigress came leaping over the bushes and went straight to Nihar, rubbing herself all over her and meowing and lying on her feet and ankles just like a little cub happy to see her Ma after a long time! After a while she rushed to Saroj, put both her paws around his neck and licked his face as if asking him where he had been. She was so obviously thrilled and happy to see them both that all the onlookers were astonished at the loving behaviour of a full-grown tigress towards her 'lost' adopted parents.

And so Khairi returned to the Kairakacha camp with the very relieved parents and made sure never to lose her way again when camping out with them.

There was only ever one tragic accident between Khairi and the other animals in the forest rest house.

Manika was a female four-horned antelope fawn who had been brought to Jashipur in June 1975 when she was about a month old. Nursed back to health by Nihar, the fawn gradually became a good friend of Khairi. She used to go out and browse in the compound of the rest house where Khairi would sometimes stalk her to take her by surprise. But she could never catch her. Like all members of her tribe, the little fawn would bounce away in a few leaps and then wait again for Khairi to catch up. This would happen again and again till Manika rushed inside through the back door and straight into Nihar's lap!

Sometimes when Nihar was not present, she would slump in her bed resigned to Khairi's designs. The tigress would lift Manika in her jaws by the small of her back and carry her out to the lawn, where she would gently lay her down on the grass and proceed to lick her all over which Manika appeared to enjoy!

It was just like this, late in the evening of December 1979, when Manika, then seven months old, came into the bedroom and lay down in her bunk. After a while, the tigress too came in and, before anybody could do anything, she went to Manika and, holding her in her jaws, ran away outside. Saroj gave her chase and finally managed to rescue the fawn whom Khairi had not intended to harm but merely wanted to play with. Surprisingly, the next evening the same thing happened all over again. But this time, when Khairi rushed outside with the fawn in her mouth, Manika's head hit resoundingly against the open door.

When Saroj found the tigress and the fawn this time, Manika's head was dangling on one side, and despite all their best efforts, she could not be revived. While the parents had to accept this hard fact, Khairi too, in her own way, showed how she felt about the accident. Time and again she would come and smell and lick Manika, as if to get her to get up and come to play. She had not meant any harm to her friend and the fact that Manika had hit her head on the door was not her fault. For many days she grieved for her friend, a fact noticed by all who knew her.

And so, we come to the end of this beautiful story about the only instance of a full-grown tigress' living among people that she'd came to love as her own—people with whom she shared all her experiences of joys and sorrows, of acceptance and loss, of giving and receiving. Belonging to a gene feared and hated for their ferocity and murderous cunning, Khairi was a model of gentle passivity to all who met her. In her short life she became famous, not only in India but abroad as well.

It was a small incident that was to prove fatal for that princess among tigresses.

On 20 February 1981, a stray dog, barely the size of a small puppy, squeezed inside the compound of the forest rest house and, before anybody could prevent it, Khairi had killed it with a bite to the neck. The dog's blood entered her mouth and coated her tongue, and when she later licked herself, the saliva carrying the virus entered her system. Unfortunately, the dog was suffering from rabies and it was the rabies virus that slowly started to infect Khairi's brain.

Saroj was then not in Similipal, having been called to Delhi for a conference, otherwise he would have certainly sent the dog's brain to the Veterinary Science College to check for rabies. Unfortunately, he returned only on March 2. At this point, the virus was still incubating and no outward symptoms had yet appeared to indicate the infection.

But as the rabies advanced in her brain, Khairi was obviously in great pain and discomfort. She could not keep down any food, milk, medicines or even water lovingly given to her by her parents, whom she clung to in her agony. Finally, when there was no chance of recovery, to save her from her further suffering, she was put down by an overdose of tranquillizers.

And so it was that Khairi, that great tigress, passed away on 28 March 1981, barely six-and-a-half-eventful-years old, having lived as a daughter of Saroj Raj Choudhury and his family. Saroj himself could not bear the separation from Khairi and succumbed to a heart attack barely a year after her premature death.

Saroj Raj Choudhury was posthumously conferred with a Padma Shri for his immense contribution to forestry and the preservation of wildlife.

History of India's Forests and Wildlife

As a young scholar of history many years ago, I used to often ask myself that if India had such a glorious history going back to the accounts given in the epics, Ramayana and Mahabharata, why were there no stone palaces or other ruins of the places mentioned in them? Surely there should be some archaeological ruins of the ancient cities of Ayodhya, Mithila, Prayagraj, Mathura, Hastinapur or Indraprastha?

Chalo, these are from too far back in time—5000 BCE or 3000 BCE—but what about more recent history? For example, in the 6th century BCE, we had the sixteen great kingdoms—or the Solasa Mahajanapada—in India: Magadha, Kashi, Kosala, Anga, Matsya and Avanti and the famous republican states, Vaishali, Saket and Shravasti. These existed at the time of the Buddha and great cities like Pataliputra, Vaishali, Kapilavastu, Ujjain or Mahishmati which are mentioned in the Buddhist, Puranic and Jain accounts have left almost no visible signs on the ground.

Or, coming to an even more relevant issue, why are there no palaces remaining of such great Indian kings as Ashoka,

Chandragupta Maurya, Harshvardhan, Samudragupta or Vikramaditya?

Elsewhere in the world we have the Parthenon as a remnant of the Greek civilization, the relics of the Roman Empire in Italy, ruins of Persepolis and Babylon, the Pyramids and the Abu Simbel Temple Complex, the Mayan and Aztec monuments, the Great Wall of China, and so on, to mark the progress of world history at different times.

In India, however, it appears that recorded history only goes back to the stone edifices dating to the 10th century CE when the Turko-Afghan invasion first established its sway over northern India and built the marvellous structures around the Qutub Minar, the Purana Qila, the Red Forts in Delhi and Agra, the mausoleum of Humayun, the Taj Mahal, etc.

Where is our forgotten past and why are we not witness to the wonder that was India? This concerned me greatly and I often fretted for an answer.

Surprisingly, the solution was given to me by Prof. David Landes, my teacher of Comparative History at Harvard University, who said to me:

'Yogesh, ancient India was a vast ocean of tropical forests. In the olden days these forests covered all of northern India till below the fertile Indo-Gangetic plains and all the cities and towns were surrounded by dense jungles. So naturally, dwelling units, even palaces and royal structures, were largely constructed of timber that would not last for centuries.'

This explanation got me thinking and I delved into our history to get an idea of the extent of the forest cover in the olden days. What I learnt surprised me.

If you read the Ramayana of Valmiki, you get an idea of

the great expanse of forests that covered virtually the whole of India in those ancient days. When the young Rama and Lakshman followed the sage Visvamitra to do battle with Taraka, Marich and Subahu, they entered a thick jungle that stretched virtually from the gates of Ayodhya all the way to the Brahmarishi's ashrama.

The epic then describes their journey to the ashrama of Gautam Rishi and on to Mithila through large tracts of forests, fording pristine rivers and not encountering any large towns or cities. They even passed the site where the great capital of Magadha, Pataliputra, would come up later, but did not seem to see any sign of it.

For the early Aryan settlers in India, apart from the capitals of the various kingdoms, the ashrams that dotted the forests, where religious studies and practices were carried out and where education was imparted to the young, were the nuclei of society, particularly rural society.

When you read of Shri Rama's journey to Chitrakoot and thence through the Dandaka Forest to Panchavati and Kishkinda, you come across many of these ashrams, their names made famous by the great Rishis who headed them—Bharadwaj, Valmiki, Atri, Sarabhanga, Sutiksna, Agastya and Sabari.

The Ramayana mentions at various places the wildlife that existed in the forests: large herds of elephants; deer of every kind; lions and tigers; bears and boars; ferocious horned wild buffaloes. The ashramas, again, were home to many tame deer, especially the black buck. From in and around Chitrakoot, which was virtually the heart of India, one gets accounts of lions, tigers, elephants, buffalo and all manner of small game and fowl.

The Mahabharata too is filled with images of luxuriant forests, which seem to cover most of northern India, from the Himalayas to the Yamuna-Gangetic and Saraswati-Sindhu basins. While Hastinapur was on the banks of the Ganga, Indraprastha lay along the Yamuna and the Yadavs followed the Saraswati to its meeting-point with the Arabian Sea at Dwarka.

For me, one of the worst stories in the Mahabharata, is the one about the burning and destruction of the Khandava Vana, the forest-land on which the city of Indraprastha, the capital of the Pandavas, was sought to be erected.

After the swayamvara of Draupadi, when the Pandavas returned to Hastinapur, Dhritarashtra and the elders in a Council decided to split the Kuru kingdom into two parts, one for Duryodhana and his brothers and the other for the Pandavas. In a public ceremony, Dhritarashtra gave the Pandavas the forest of Khandavaprastha and asked them to make their new home there.

The place offered to the Pandavas was a piece of wildland far away from the capital city of Hastinapur. It was the duty of the king, Yudhishthira, to build the new city, Indraprastha, there and to consolidate the land to make it liveable for his citizens. Sadly, for it to prosper, Khandava Vana would have to be levelled and agriculture established in its place.

But the manner in which it was done was horrifying. We are told that, aided by the Fire God, Agni, the Pandavas encircled the forest and ruthlessly burnt everything to a crisp. A great slaughter followed. The warriors went around in their chariots, killing anything that tried to escape the blazing inferno: lions, elephants, deer, monkeys, serpents, all manner of birds and, they say, even bees.

It is described as a remorseless, unsparing and merciless carnage. None of the animals were given a chance to escape, they were relentlessly slain or thrown back into the flames when they tried to escape the fire to save their lives.

Indraprastha would forever bear the mark of this senseless cruelty, and who knows, the later events in the capital could have been a fallout of this act of great adharma, the reverberations of which are perhaps being felt to this day.

But the forests still held their sway, and right up to the time of the invasion of Alexander in 326 BCE ,the jungles in India were looked at with trepidation by the invaders. By this time, the elephants too had become formidable engines of war.

The number of elephants employed in the service of war alone was staggering. When Porus confronted Alexander on the banks of the Jhelum in May 326 BCE, his army comprised 200 elephants, which were placed at the head of the formation and were flanked by infantry on both sides and then by chariots. Curtius, the Greek writer, tells us that since the foreign invaders were facing elephants in war for the first time, they were quite terror-stricken by the sight of the fully armoured beasts charging at them. It was unfortunate for Porus that there had been torrential rain the night before, which prevented his elephants from rivalling the speed of the cavalry. He was therefore soon forced to retreat. On such inconsequential details is the tapestry of history woven!

By the time of Chandragupta Maurya and the Mauryan Empire, the role of the elephant as a key element in the war machinery was already well-established. Special forests were set apart for elephants. The killing of elephants was made punishable by death and the nature of their training as instruments of war was comprehensibly defined.

Chanakya's *Arthashastra* is worth quoting at length in this regard:

> In the extreme limit of the country, elephant forests, separated from wild tracts, shall be formed.
>
> The superintendent of forests with his retinue of forest guards shall not only maintain the up-keep of the forests, but also acquaint himself with all passages for entrance into, or exit from such of them as are mountainous or boggy or contain rivers or lakes.
>
> Whoever kills an elephant shall be put to death.
>
> Whoever brings in the pair of tusks of an elephant, dead from natural causes, shall receive a reward of four-and-a-half panas.
>
> Guards of elephant forests, assisted by those who rear elephants, those who enchain the legs of elephants, those who guard the boundaries, those who live in forests, as well as by those who nurse elephants, shall, with the help of five or seven female elephants to help in tethering wild ones, trace the whereabouts of herds of elephants by following the course of urine and dungs left by elephants and along forest-tracts covered over with branches, and by observing the spots where elephants slept or sat before or left dungs, or where they had just destroyed the banks of rivers or lakes. They shall also precisely ascertain whether any mark is due to the movements of elephants in herds, of an elephant roaming single, of a stray elephant, of a leader of herds, of a tusker, of a rogue elephant, of an

elephant in rut, of a young elephant, or of an elephant that has escaped from the cage.

Experts in catching elephants shall follow the instructions given to them by the elephant doctor and catch such elephants as are possessed of auspicious characteristics and good character.

The victory of kings (in battles) depends mainly upon elephants; for elephants, being of large bodily frame, are capable not only to destroy the arrayed army of an enemy, his fortifications, and encampments, but also to undertake works that are dangerous to life.

The Superintendent of elephants shall take proper steps to protect elephant-forests and supervise the operations with regard to the standing or lying in stables of elephants, male, female, or young, when they are tired after training, and examine the proportional quantity of rations and grass, the extent of training given to them, their accoutrements and ornaments, as well as the work of elephant-doctors, of trainers of elephants in warlike feats, and of grooms, such as drivers, binders and others.

Elephants are classified into four kinds in accordance with the training they are given: that which is tame able, that which is trained for war, that which is trained for riding, and rogue elephants.

Those which are tame able fall under five groups: that which suffers a man to sit on its withers, that which allows itself to be tethered to a post, that which can be taken to water, that which lies in pits, and that which is attached to its herd.

All these elephants shall be treated with as much care as a young elephant.[2]

For the first eight years of his reign, Asoka followed the lifestyle of Chandragupta until, in the ninth year, he embarked on the conquest of Kalinga. It was to mark the turning point in his life, for the trauma of death and suffering caused by the war so revolted him that he swore to abjure all form of killing and violence from there onwards.

For the rest of his life, Asoka stood for the religion of ahimsa or non-violence to men and animals—something that he preached through many of his edicts. The unrestricted slaughter of animals for the royal table was first limited to one deer and two peacocks, and even this was later totally abolished.

Asoka made repeated requests in his edicts that animals be treated with kindness and care. The Fifth Pillar Edict contained a detailed list of animals that were not to be killed under any circumstances, and a further list of animals and creatures which were declared inviolable on certain days. Forests were not to be cut or set on fire and special forests were to be set apart for the breeding of elephants (nagavanas).

Asoka abolished the time-honoured royal sport of hunting in which his grandfather had indulged with so much pomp and heraldry. He also banned the cruel fights between animals as public sporting events.

For the first time in its long-recorded history, India got

[2]Kautilya, *Arthashastra,* R. Shamasastry (trans.), Government Press, Bangalore, 1915, 65–66.

a real-time example of state-enforced forest and wildlife preservation and a shining example of what should be an ideal ecological policy. But alas, this was too good to last and the Asokan ideal was demolished with the death of the great emperor.

Looking back over the pages of India's history after the era of the Mauryas and Guptas, there have been three clearly defined periods that have had a deleterious impact on the immense forests and wildlife in the country. The first was the influx and conquest of the land by the Muslim invaders from the North-West, particularly the Mughals. This was closely followed by British colonial rule and its offspring, the Princely States, and, finally, the initial years of India's Independence.

For the Mughals, hunting was an ingrained habit. It was perceived as a royal prerogative which allowed them to exercise authority over nature, gather local information and, at the same time, overawe their subjects. They had a variety of hunting techniques which they used in their shikargahs to hunt not only big game such as rhinoceros, elephants, lions and tigers—which were seen as imperial entitlement— but also black buck, deer, nilgais, boars, wild ass and buffalo, apart from sundry smaller game and birds.

Babur first showed Humayun a rhinoceros in the jungles around Peshawar and observed how many of them they were at that place. Gulbadan Begum, Humayun's aunt and biographer, commented how this became a favourite sport and hunting area for Humayun in later years.

While the Mughal emperors created special shikargahs for their hunts, they also used a variety of hunting techniques borrowed from their ancestors. One of the most abhorrent in terms of the manner of killing was the qamargha, or ring-hunt. This involved driving thousands of animals from surrounding areas into a specially created and steadily constricting circular enclosure formed by fences, screens, nets and human chains, where the frightened animals would then be mercilessly slaughtered in the thousands.

A monumental qamargha was organized for Akbar around Lahore in 1567, for which over 15,000 animals were driven in from neighbouring hills for over a month by 50,000 beaters into a circle sixteen kilometres in circumference, which had been created especially for the hunt.

Emperor Jahangir, not to be left behind, proudly recounts that, by the eleventh year of his accession, 28,532 heads of game were taken in his presence. Of these, 17,167 animals, including 86 tigers, 889 nilgai or blue bulls, 1,670 rams, and sundry other deer, wolves, chinkara, chital, mountain goats, wild buffaloes, pigs, wild asses and over 13,964 birds were killed by him alone.[3]

Up to the time of the Mughals, and well into the eighteenth century, India's forest cover had remained pretty much intact. The great Terai belt of forest, running along the Indo-Nepal border extended from north Bihar to much of eastern Uttar Pradesh and Rohilkhand and past the Siwalik hills right up to the flood plains of the river Indus. Tavernier wrote of the region around Gorakhpur being 'full of forests' in the middle of the seventeenth century.[4]

[3] *Tuzuk-e-Jahangiri*, Alexander Rogers (trans.), D.K. Publishers, New Delhi, 167.

[4] Tavernier, Jean-Baptiste, *Travels in India: Vol. II*, V. Ball (trans.), W. Crooke (ed.), London, 1925.

The southern parts of the plains of the Indus was largely scrub land or enclosed by the desert as it is even today. These extended from the Punjab, Rajasthan, Gujarat and Sindh up to Saurashtra. This area was home to the cheetahs, lions and wild asses and many of the imperial hunting grounds of the Mughals were located here.

The most extensive unbroken stretch of forest in Mughal times, much of which has survived to this day, was in Central India, extending from Orissa through Bastar, Bihar, southern Bundelkhand and Madhya Pradesh right up to Gujarat. Irfan Habib has termed this the 'Great Central Indian Forest'. The forest belt extended down the Western Ghats to the tip of Kerala and covered most of Karnataka and Andhra Pradesh along the beds of the Krishna-Tungabhadra and Godavari rivers. Large herds of elephants, tigers and all manner of game were found in the rich teak, sandalwood, rosewood and other exotic timber forests in these places.

Delhi lay at the foothills of the Aravalli range and was home to some of the most prized shikargahs under the Mughals. Its outlying areas—like Palam, Mehrauli, Najafgarh and Hauz Khas—were famous for their large antelope, leopard and tiger populations, while the extensive riverside khadar to the north and east was the natural habitat of a variety of game.

> In the neighborhoods of Agra and Delhi, along the course of the Gemna, reaching to the mountains, and even on both sides of the road leading to Lahor, there is a large quantity of uncultivated land, covered either with copse wood or with grasses six feet high. All this land is guarded with utmost vigilance; and excepting

partridges, quails, and hares, which the natives catch with nets, no person, be he who he may, is permitted to disturb the game, which is consequently very abundant.[5]

Abu'l Fazl notes that elephants were found in large numbers in the provinces of Agra, parts of Berar, Allahabad, Malwa, Bihar, Bengal and Orissa.[6]

The semi-arid regions of western and central India were the most fertile regions for hunting the cheetah. Pakpattan, Bhatinda, Bhatnair, Nagaur, Merta, Jhunjhunu, Dholpur and Hissar Firuza are all mentioned as shikargah-i muqarrars for providing great quantities of cheetahs.

In 1624, Jahangir used a lion hunt in Mathura as an opportunity to flush out farmers who had used the protection of thick jungles to indulge in acts of defiance by refusing to pay taxes to the jagirdars and to commit highway robbery.[7] Bari in Dholpur was a famous shikargah where Jehangir was attacked by a lion and only saved by the valiant intervention of Anup Rai and Prince Khurram, the future Shah Jehan. Jehangir also refers admiringly to the Empress Nur Jehan shooting a tiger in the vicinity of Mathura.

---

[5]Bernier, François, *Travels in the Mogul Empire,* Archibald Constable (trans.), Oxford University Press, London, 1983, 375.

[6]Allami, Abul Fazl, *Ain-i-Akbari, Vol. I,* H. Blochmann (trans.), D.C. Phillott (ed.), Vols. II and III, H.S. Jarrett (trans.), Jadunath Sarkar (ed.), Asiatic Society, Kolkata, 2010.

[7]*Tuzuk-e-Jahangiri,* Alexander Rogers (trans.), D.K. Publishers, New Delhi, 412.

The forests surrounding the water bodies around Hissar and Karnal also had a great concentration of game for the chase, such as antelopes and nilgais, and were particularly famous as cheetah terrain, an animal that could be trained to hunt alongside the emperor. The thick forests along the river Brahmaputra in Assam, and more generally in the Northeast, were home to all manner of game, especially wild elephants, rhinoceros, tiger and deer, which remained virtually untouched till the arrival of the British who started to exploit the timber commercially and started planting tea gardens in the foothills.

The Mughal penchant for cutting vast swathes of forests that hindered the movement of troops and their love of hunting resulted in the absolute decimation of wildlife in different parts of the subcontinent. Many rich breeding grounds of elephants were destroyed; the great Indian one-horned rhinoceros disappeared from the Indus Valley; the cheetah teetered on the brink of extinction and the majestic lion became confined to the western extremities of Rajasthan, Gujarat and Saurashtra.

This was to prove the afterglow of the day; the sunset was fast approaching.

When the British first established their hold on India, first in Bengal, Carnatic and then slowly over the rest of the country, they were confronted by the country's vast forests and, for them, its terrifying beasts—tigers, elephants, snakes, wild buffaloes and lions, which seemed to be the carrier of dreaded diseases like malaria, typhoid and cholera.

The gloom of the forests had to be cleared, in part because timber was required for building ships and wooden ties for railway lines, but also because land was needed for growing commercial crops like cotton, tea, coffee, cardamom, rubber, spices and opium. Animals that destroyed these crops would necessarily have to be culled, so hunting acquired a new prestige. Sporting and hunting were an ancient tradition linked to the aristocracy in England. This was now carried to India as a marker of identity separating the colonizer from the colonized.

Generations of young British recruits inducted into India were brought up on the idea that hunting was a gentleman's sport and that India's forests were a sportsman's paradise that provided unlimited opportunities to pursue and kill wild animals. Hunting was a sign of being seen as a pukkasahib, and the ability to hunt became a distinguishing mark of aristocratic privilege that attended the right to rule.

Hunting was also presented as a way of protecting the 'natives' from the ravages of 'savage beasts'. Animals were thus termed as vermin and game that had to be exterminated in order to preserve peace in the countryside. Rewards were announced for destruction of carnivores which included rewards for killing tigers (Rs 7), leopards (Rs 5) and others such as bear, hyena and wolf (Rs 3).

The ninety years between the establishment of Crown rule in India post the Great Uprising of 1857 and India's Independence in 1947 saw a marked change in the forest cover of the country and its wildlife population. Gone forever were the great herds of wild elephants in the dwindling forests of the Sundarbans, Nilgiris and Central Indian plains.

Gone too were all signs of the rhinoceros from North India, who were now confined to the Brahmaputra basin in Assam. Lions were now extinct in all parts of the country except Gujarat and the feline grace of the cheetah would forever be lost to the subcontinent.

According to Mahesh Rangarajan, over 80,000 tigers, more than 150,000 leopards and 200,000 wolves were slaughtered in the fifty years between 1875 and 1925.[8]

Following on the heels of the British were the maharajas and princes of the erstwhile semi-independent princely states. They reserved the right to hunt in their territories. However, stories abound of their organizing, with pomp and splendour, elaborate hunts for their colonial masters. Kings and queens, archdukes, presidents and viceroys, political and district officers were often royal invitees.

As Mahesh Rangarajan has remarked, 'In the annals of the hunt, the Indian princes stand out in a league of their own. Despite recent attempts to rewrite their role as precursors of modern-day conservation, their record was not always an edifying one.'[9]

While any wild animal was fit as game, Cooch Bihar, for instance, killed over 200 rhinos; special ire was directed at the most sublime of all animals—the tiger.

---

[8]Rangarajan, Mahesh, *India's Wildlife History*, Permanent Black, New Delhi, 2001, 32.

[9]Ibid., 36.

The following is a distressing litany of killing of tigers by members of the royalty[10]:

Member of royalty	*No. of tigers killed*
Col. Kesri Singh in his tenure as Shikarkhana in charge of Jaipur and Gwalior	1,000
Maharao Raja Bahadur Singh of Bundi	200
Maharao Raja Raghubir Singh of Bundi	100
Maharaja Ganesh Pal Deo of Karauli	300
Yuvraj Surendra Pal Deo of Karauli	70
Thakur Chaggan Singh Bania of Karauli	2,000
Between 1920 and 1965 shot in Kota State	334
Maharao Bhim Singh II of Kota	300
Nawab of Tonk Nawab Saadat Ali Khan	330
Nawab Ismail Ali Khan of Tonk	130
Nawab Ibrahim Ali Khan of Tonk	120
Sahibzada Abdul Shakoor Khan of Tonk	105
Maharana Fateh Singh of Mewar	375
Maharaja Ramanuj Saran Singh Deo of Surguja	1,100

When India became independent, it was a joyous occasion for the people of the country, but not for India's wildlife. Indeed, for them, matters had become even worse because now hunters could operate within a newfound paradigm where no rules applied. So, people everywhere happily

[10]Ibid., 38; Figures taken from: Singh, Priya, *Lost Tigers: Plundered Forests*, January 2017, WWF India.

applied for arms and were at a liberty to shoot wherever and at whatever they wanted.

Within the forests proper, there was still some semblance of regulation. Shooting permits were given out for specific forest blocks on payment, permitting shooting only in the second half of the month. The permits specified the number and type of animals allowed to be shot but, invariably, the game was never confined to this number. I have seen hunting camps where huge parties were organized, with no limits being observed on the animals killed. Rules apart, most of the shooting was done from vehicles at night, so that the harsh glare of spotlights would be trained on the poor and bewildered animals.

A large number of commercial shooting companies came up, many of them floated by registered tour operators, advertising abroad for hunting in India, the special focus being on the tiger. These companies employed highly paid agents in many of the forest districts for organizing shikar. This system which guaranteed kills for the clients, often also roped in local villagers and forest officials for this task. It was calibrated slaughter, with money no object because of the profits being generated.

If this was the situation within the so-called reserved forests, the conditions in the farms adjacent to the jungle were even more abysmal. Here the farmers guarded their crops with a full license to kill any game that ventured onto their fields. The urban elite soon discovered that this was even better than getting permits to shoot in the forest blocks. Wild animals driven by hunger were bound to come to the pasture-land where they could then be mowed down by the hunters under the garb of saving farmers' crops.

Between 1950 and 1970, there was a virtual free for all as wild animals were systematically hunted down all over the country. As late as in 1963, I had witnessed a herd of over 150 black buck roaming around Akbar's mausoleum in Sikandra near Agra, or an equally large herd of swamp-deer or barasingha in the Kishenpur forest block in Lakhimpur Kheri. Soon these would disappear, as meat and trophy hunters began to ravage their numbers. My own experiences in Pilibhit district were a testimony to this awful realization. In these two decades alone, India lost a half to one-third of its wildlife inhabitants. While at the turn of the century the country still had over 40,000 tigers, by the 1970s this number had come down to less than 3,000.

But all was not lost as yet. True, the cheetah was now extinct in India—the last three being shot by the Maharaja of Surguja—and the tiger and rhino populations were on their last legs, but India's conservationists, bureaucrats and, most importantly, politicians were now awakening to the depredation being visited upon wildlife and ecology.

It needed but one powerful person to provide the lead and that pioneer was the late prime minister Indira Gandhi. M.K. Ranjit Sinhji in his book *A Life with Wildlife*, describes how he, as Deputy Secretary of Forests and Wildlife in the Ministry of Food and Agriculture in the Government of India, prepared The Wild Life (Protection) Act, 1972, under her authority and direction so that it became a pathbreaking law within a very short time.[11]

[11]Ranjitsinh, M.K., *A Life with Wildlife*, HarperCollins, Noida, 2017.

The Act paved the way for forests and wildlife to come under the Concurrent List (1976) and provided for the setting up of national parks and sanctuaries where animals would not be allowed to be hunted. It created six schedules which gave varying degrees of protection to classes of flora and fauna. Schedule I and Schedule II (Part II) got absolute protection and offences under these schedules attracted the maximum penalties.

A National Board for Wildlife was constituted as a statutory organization to act as an advisory board that offered guidance to the Central/State governments on issues of wildlife conservation in India. The Act also provided for the establishment of a National Tiger Conservation Authority to strengthen tiger conservation in India.

For the first time after Independence, a serious attempt had been made to bring forests and wildlife under a protective umbrella. How much it succeeded can be judged from the latest record of tiger preservation.

The National Tiger Conservation Authority (NTCA), in collaboration with State Forest Departments, conservation NGOs and the Wildlife Institute of India (WII), has conducted a national assessment of the 'Status of Tigers' every four years since 2006. The fourth cycle of the assessment was undertaken in 2018 and 2019, using the best available science, technology and analytical tools.

While in 2006 the tiger population had gone down to 1,411 for the whole of India, it had increased marginally to 1,706 by 2010. After four years, in 2014, the number was 2,226 and in the survey of 2018, it had grown to 2,967.

This is but a small start—there has been a growth of a mere 6 per cent per annum since 2006. The number of tigers are certainly nowhere near the number that roamed the wilds earlier on. But at least a realization has now dawned on the people of the country about how close this beautiful animal had come to becoming extinct.

Poaching and illegal hunting still exists, even in the parks and sanctuaries, as witnessed in Sariska not too long ago, and organized gangs of killers still operate in Kaziranga and even in Corbett. The continuing decline in tiger numbers in the states of Chhattisgarh and Odisha is obviously a matter of concern. Shockingly, no tigers were recorded in Buxa (West Bengal), Dampa (Mizoram) and Palamau (Jharkhand) tiger reserves. Law and order needs strengthening in these places and community social groups need to be greatly activated.

Another matter of concern is that a recent report, *Status of Tigers, Co-predators and Prey in India (2018),* has pointed out that one in every three tigers in India lives outside reserves, highlighting the challenge of protecting the animal and reducing instances of man-animal conflict. The proportion has increased from 2014, when one in every four tigers were found to be living outside reserves. Currently, the tiger population within reserves is 1,923, which means that 35 per cent of the population still resides outside of tiger reserves.

Epilogue

When I first started writing this book, I did not know it would end up delving into the history and current status of wildlife in India. It was more meant to be reminiscences of what were, many decades ago, my own personal experiences in the beautiful forests of India and the awesome animals that lived there.

Willy-nilly, I came to read the masterly accounts of India's wildlife by people who had devoted their lives to close encounters with the denizens of the jungles and had written scholarly tomes on them—people like Mahesh Rangarajan, Divyabhanusinh Chavda, Valmik Thapar, M.K. Ranjitsinhji, Jim Corbett, Fateh Singh Rathore, P.D. Stracey and countless others. Many of them were personally known to me and others like Corbett had been my bedside reading companions for a long time.

Nothing that I wrote could even remotely match what they had researched and personally gained knowledge of, through a lifetime devoted to the wild.

Mahesh Rangarajan's history of India's wildlife is still the authoritative work on the subject. Valmik Thapar and

Fateh Singh Rathore lived and breathed with tigers for many years in the Ranthambore National Park. Divyabhanusinh's story of Asia's lions is a consummate account of this majestic animal's interaction with human beings in Asia. His book *The End of a Trail: The Cheetah in India* was a pathbreaking story of a species which, sadly, is now extinct in the country, as is, unfortunately, his book on the subject.

M.K. Ranjitsinhji was a colleague of mine in college. While in the Indian Administrative Service, he had, under the directions of the then prime minister of India Indira Gandhi, composed and shepherded The Wildlife Protection Act, 1972, India's first legislation to protect the country's vanishing wildlife. It was a landmark in India's ecological awakening.

P.D. Stracey served as Chief Conservator of Forests, Assam, when I met him in the early fifties. He was a friend of my father's and lived next to us in the cantonment at Shillong. I still remember his mesmerizing accounts of elephants and Kheda operations in the hills above the Brahmaputra. In appreciation of his lifelong services, the Board of Trustees of the World Wildlife Fund has included him, along with nine other conservationists, in its Roll of Honor.

These were all giants of their times and did much to bring home to the people of the country, newly awakened to Independence, the wealth that existed in our forests and plains.

To their accounts, I could only add the impressions of a novice freshly recruited into government and luckily assigned to districts that had a wealth of forests and wildlife. In a way I straddled two worlds, the old and the new: the old India a remnant of colonial darkness, of white Sahibs and brown subjects, of dynastic Maharajas resplendent in their bejewelled pomp and glory while their subjects lived in abject poverty, just a step ahead of famine and disease, of forests teeming with wildlife of every sort and empty jungles, verdant as ever, but bare and lonely with life extinguished in them.

At first I tended to blame the princes and their cohorts, though many of them became great personal friends: Bhawani Singh of Jaipur (Bubbles), then a Major in the Para Brigade in Agra, with whom I spent many an evening in the local club and the Brigade Mess; Maharaj Gaj Singh (Baapji) of Jodhpur and Arvind Singh of Mewar who were mentors when I was in the Tourism Ministry, and of course Madhavrao Scindia of Gwalior, the finest minister I had the privilege of serving under while in the Department of Tourism and Civil Aviation.

True, many of the ruling classes were avid hunters, but as Divyabhanusinh pointed out to me in a private correspondence:

> Some were chronic destroyers: Cooch Bihar-200 plus rhinos, Sarguja-1100 tigers. But the princes by and large did not allow anyone to shoot in their reserves—a tradition going back to Kautilya. The shooters were only themselves and those they permitted. Thus, the forests and grasslands got protected. After independence it became a free for all. Today we have some 600 plus NPs and Sanctuaries. I would not be surprised if most of these are former princely preserves. For example: Gir-Junagadh, Mityala-Bhavnagar, Vansda NP-Bansda, Hingolgadh-Jasdan, Radhanagri-Kolhapur, Similipal-

> Mayurbhanj, Ranthambore-Jaipur, Sariska-Alwar, Keola Deo-Bharatpur, Kela Devi-Karauli, Jaisamand-Udaipur, Gajner-Bikaner, Bandipur and Nagarhole-Mysore, and Periyar-Travancore—the list is endless.

But the same cannot be said of the shikaris and shikar companies that came up after Independence. The sheer commercialization of shikar, or hunting for hunting's sake, became a new lexicon in the country's jargon as people demanded, and were given, arms to ostensibly defend themselves. This was different from the need to protect crops and promote agriculture. While there is always something to be said of real man-animal conflict with weighty arguments on either side, and I was an inadvertent witness to this struggle, the wanton slaughter of animals for food or trophy, that goes under the detestable title of shikar, is something else: it is slaughter of defenceless animals just for satisfying one's bloodlust. I have always been sickened by photographs of our so-called 'great hunters' showing how many tigers, leopards, elephants and other game they have killed—a la the Mughal emperors. But sadly, this indiscriminate killing was permitted, and once upon a time had even been applauded.

But, as it happens so often, perceptions tend to change.

Today shikar is looked down upon and hunting is associated mostly with criminals and poachers. There are many social groups now, especially among our villagers, such as the Bishnoi community, who are devoted to protecting wildlife.

I was immensely proud when Vikram, as a television anchor, came together with the legendary Amitabh Bachchan, another friend from college days, to do a programme with Aircel on the Save our Tigers campaign. They roped in many chief ministers of states, politicians, bureaucrats and NGOs, who campaigned for the need to protect the tiger and conserving our ecological heritage. It is events such as this that will contribute to preserving our priceless environmental heritage, and who knows, India may well again see its forests and plains alive with the sound of music.

Glossary

Aayah	Maid servant or nursemaid
Angavastra	A piece of cloth draped over the shoulders, often worn by men
Baapji	An honorific term meaning 'father' or 'respected elder'
Bania	Trader or merchant, usually of a business caste
Barasingha	Twelve-tined swamp deer
Barkhurdar	Literally 'son'; used either affectionately or sarcastically
Behar	Ravine terrain along the river Chambal
Chaddar	A sheet or covering cloth placed over a shrine or sacred site
Charpoi	Traditional woven bed made of jute or cotton rope
Chillum	Earthenware pipe used for smoking tobacco or other substances
Chinkara	Indian gazelle

Chital	Spotted deer
Chowkidar	Watchman or security guard
Chunni	A long scarf or stole worn over the shoulders and head
Daroga	Police inspector or officer in charge of a police station
Darshan	Opportunity to behold or have a sighting of a deity or revered person
Dekchis	Cooking pots or utensils
Dhoti	Traditional male garment draped around the waist and legs
Diya	Small cup-shaped oil lamp made of baked clay
Ghati	Steps or banks leading down to a river, ghats
Hanuman Chalisa	Hymn consisting of forty verses in praise of Lord Hanuman
Holi	Festival of colours marking the arrival of spring
Jagirdars	Holder of a feudal land grant, jagir
Jhala	Village dwelling or homestead
Jhola	Cloth shoulder bag or sling bag
Kadhai	Large iron vessel used *for fry*ing or boiling sugarcane juice
Kakkar	Barking deer, see also Muntjac
Kakker	Swamp partridge, variant spelling of Kakkar also used locally

Kandis	Cow-dung cakes mixed with straw, used as cooking fuel
Kata	Young male buffalo calf
Khaleej	Pheasant, also called Khalij Pheasant
Kharif	Summer or monsoon crop
Kheer	Sweetened milk and rice pudding
Kutcha	Temporary or unfinished structure, road or material
Lambardar	Village headman or revenue collector
Langurs	Black-faced monkeys
Lassi	Sweet or salted drink made from yoghurt and water
Machan	Elevated platform or seat built on a tree, usually for watching or hunting animals
Mahout	Elephant keeper or rider
Maiya	Mother; often used affectionately or reverentially
Malguzar	Landowner or rent collector
Malkhana	Armoury or storage for seized goods in a police station
Mofussil	Rural or provincial area (outside major towns)
Mundha	Small bamboo stool or perch used for sitting
Nadi	River
Narkul	Tall water reed or bulrush found in marshes
Nilgai	Blue bull antelope

Nullah	Watercourse, ravine or drainage channel
Phoot lo	Colloquial phrase meaning 'run along', 'buzz off' or 'make yourself scarce'
Pradhan	Village head or elected leader of a panchayat
Prasad	Sacred food offering made to a deity and later distributed to devotees
Pucca Sahib	Term for a high-ranking or authoritative Englishman during colonial times
Qamargha	Traditional hunting technique in which animals are driven by beaters towards hunters in a ring formation
Qanungo	Revenue official responsible for maintaining land records
Rabi	Winter crop
Sambar	Large brown deer found in Indian forests
Sher	Tiger
Shikar	Hunting or game hunting
Shikargahs	Hunting lodge or retreat
Shikari	Hunter
Swayamvara	Ceremony in which a woman chooses her husband from assembled suitors
Taqavi	Cash grant or government loan given to villagers in times of distress
Tattoo	Small indigenous horse, typically used for riding or transport in rural India
Tehsildar	Revenue officer and head of a local tehsil, sub-district

Terai	Belt of forest and marshland at the foothills of the Himalayas
Tharus	Indigenous tribal community of the Terai region
Tilak	Sacred vermilion or sandalwood mark applied to the forehead
Zamindar	Landowner or landlord who leases land to tenants

Bibliography

Allami, Abul Fazl. *Ain-i-Akbari, Vol. I,* H. Blochmann (trans.), D.C. Phillott (ed.), Vols. II and III, H.S. Jarrett (trans.), Jadunath Sarkar (ed.). Asiatic Society, 2010.

Bernier, François. *Travels in the Mogul Empire,* Archibald Constable (trans.). Oxford University Press, 1983.

Corbett, Jim. *Jungle Lore.* Oxford University Press, 1953.

Corbett, Jim. *Man-Eaters of Kumaon.* Oxford University Press, 2008.

Corbett, Jim. *The Temple Tiger.* Oxford University Press, 1988.

Divyabhanusinh, A. *The End of a Trail: The Cheetah in India.* Oxford University Press, 1999.

Divyabhanusinh, A. (ed.). *The Lions of India.* Orient Blackswan, 2011.

Divyabhanusinh, A. *The Story of Asia's Lions.* The Marg Foundation, 2008.

Divyabhanusinh, A., Ashok Kumar Das, and Shibani Bose. *The Story of India's Unicorns.* The Marg Foundation, 2018.

Kautilya. *Arthashastra,* R. Shamasastry (trans.). Government Press, 1915.

Majumdar, R.C. (ed.). *The Age of Imperial Unity, Volume II.* Bharatiya Vidya Bhavan, 1980.

Pye-Smith, Charlie. *In Search of Wild India.* UBS Publishers, 1992.

Rangarajan, Mahesh. *India's Wildlife History.* Orient Blackswan, 2006.

Ranjitsinh, M.K. *A Life with Wildlife.* HarperCollins, 2017.

Sankhala, Kailash. *Tiger.* Simon and Schuster, 1977.

Singh, Priya. *Lost Tigers, Plundered Forests.* WWF India, 2017.

Stracey, P.D. *Elephant Gold.* Natraj Publishers, 1963.

Tavernier, Jean-Baptiste. *Travels in India: Vol. II,* V. Ball (trans.), William Crooke (ed.). Oxford University Press, 1925.

Thapar, Valmik. *Living with Tigers.* Aleph Book Company, 2016.

Thapar, Valmik. *Tiger Fire.* Aleph Book Company, 2013.

Thapar, Valmik, and Fateh Singh Rathore. *Tigers: The Secret Life.* Elm Tree Books, 1989.

Tuzuk-e-Jahangiri, Alexander Rogers (trans.). D.K. Publishers.